# THE ASTROLOGICAL COOKBOOK

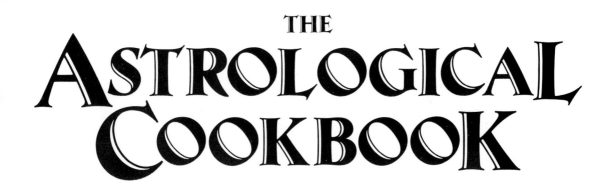

## Your Culinary Guide to Celestial Harmony

### by Rana Birkmeier

A Bluewood Book

This edition was produced
and published in 1994
by Bluewood Books,
A Division of The Siyeh
Investment Group, Inc.
P.O. Box 460313
San Francisco, CA 94146

ISBN 0-912517-11-5

Printed in Hong Kong

Designed by Tom Debolski

Edited by Ruth DeJauregui
and Bill Yenne

When preparing meals for yourself, or for friends,
always be aware that personal dislikes and food
allergies are also an important consideration in the
preparation of a truly harmonious meal. No
person can achieve celestial harmony if they are
allergic to a particular food or a particular spice.

# CONTENTS

# PREFACE

## By John Carlos Rehervidas
### Director and Founder, Institute for Astrological Research

Just as the planets guide our greater destiny, the food we eat governs the inner well-being of our bodies, our minds and our spirit. Our ancestors understood this and, in recent years, we have been discovering these aspects of our being.

What many people do not understand, however, is that there is a direct correlation between our celestial and our physical well-being. What we eat is just as much part of our being in harmony with the universe as where our Mercury or Saturn is.

Noted astrologer Rana Birkmeier has brought these together again in what will surely be one of the most important cookbooks of the decade. She has carefully studied legends and traditions associated with astrology and has compiled a wonderful collection of recipes that allow us to stay in harmony with the cosmos while enjoying the fruits of the Earth. Indeed, Rana has provided us with a wondrous cornucopia of delicious recipes.

Never before has there been such a fabulous cookbook that is also a complete and in-depth study of the special foods associated with each astrological sign. Rana has even gone a step further, as she specifies the spices associated each of the three Decans within each of the twelve signs. Her book is destined to be a milestone.

Through the ages, food has always been more than mere nourishment. Meals have always had their ritual aspects.

Important days in ancient and medieval calendars were referred to as "feast days" and *THE ASTROLOGICAL COOKBOOK* continues this tradition.

Rana peels away the complex mysteries of astrologic cooking and makes it fun and interesting to enjoy and to share.

# INTRODUCTION

## by Rana Birkmeier

Two of the most important things affecting the modern woman and man—just as they were important to ancient woman and man—are the way that the planets guide our greater destiny, and the way the food we eat governs the inner well-being of our bodies, our minds and our spirit.

Our ancestors knew and understood this, but just as so many aspects of ancient knowledge were stamped out, so too was our instinctive understanding that our astrological affiliation is just as important to our true identity as our gender, our race or our nationality. Leos are Leos and nothing can make them a Pisces.

It has been said that you are what you eat. This is true. The foods that each of us eat are an integral part of our identity, but for the most part, we, as a culture, have forgotten *why*. I have prepared this book to address this obvious omission in our contemporary literature.

What we have done in *THE ASTROLOGICAL COOKBOOK* is to include special recipes for every sign of the Zodiac, as well as specific spices associated with each of the three Decans within each of the twelve signs. Many of these recipes have been with us for many years, and some date back to the nineteenth century. Some were created only yesterday, using age-old astrological principles.

Just as each sign of the Zodiac is linked to one of the four cardinal elements—earth, air, water, fire—so too is each sign linked to a particular nouriture, or primal form of nourishment. Just as each of the twelve signs is ruled by a specific planet, so too is there a specific cornucopia of fruits of the Earth that are related to each of the signs by way of the ruling planets.

However, when preparing meals for yourself, or for friends, always be aware that personal dislikes and food allergies are also an important consideration in the preparation of a truly harmonious meal. No person can achieve celestial harmony if they are allergic to a particular food or a particular spice.

| | Ruling Element | Ruling Planet | Nouriture |
|---|---|---|---|
| **Aries** | Fire | Mars | Lamb, Mutton, Goat |
| **Taurus** | Earth | Venus | Beef |
| **Gemini** | Air | Mercury | Fowl |
| **Cancer** | Water | Moon | Crab |
| **Leo** | Fire | Sun | Wild Game |
| **Virgo** | Earth | Mercury | Veal |
| **Libra** | Air | Venus | Cornucopia |
| **Scorpio** | Water | Mars | Shellfish |
| **Sagittarius** | Fire | Jupiter | Ham, Pork, Sausages |
| **Capricorn** | Earth | Saturn | Lamb |
| **Aquarius** | Air | Saturn | Seafood |
| **Pisces** | Water | Jupiter | Fish |

Just as personal likes and dislikes play an important role in modifying a strict astrologically appropriate menu, so too do similarities between signs. Just as several signs share a ruling planet, so too do some signs share certain fruits, vegetables and nuts. Further, the nouriture of Aries is similar to that of Capricorn and the nouriture of Scorpio is similar to that of Aquarius. As such, many recipes are interchangeable within these pairs. Meanwhile, many of Leo's recipes can be adapted for use by Taurus and vice versa.

By using this information, the reader can organize all aspects of a meal around the foods relating to a specific sign or group of signs. For example, a meal for a group of people might be designed around the nouriture associated with all members of the group and shared to create harmony within the group. On a more intimate scale, harmony between two lovers can also be achieved over a special meal. For example, a man may prepare a main dish associated with a his lover's sign and when he serves it to her, he may achieve particular celestial symmetry with her if it is seasoned with the herbs or spices associated with his Decan of his own sign. At the bottom of all this is, of course, our desire and inner need to be in harmony with the universe, with those around us and with our own being through the food that nourishes our physical bodies.

*Bon Appetit!*

# ARIES

## March 21 through April 19

| Ruling Element | Ruling Planet | Nouriture |
|:---:|:---:|:---:|
| **Fire** | **Mars** | **Lamb, Mutton, Goat** |

As an Aries, you are quick-witted, creative and a bit impetuous. Unless you have chosen to lead a vegetarian life, Lamb, Mutton, or Goat are your choices for a main dish. You enjoy a good time and friends. Since Hops are one of your vegetables, you may enjoy a good beer now and then.

Just as the lifestyle that Aries people enjoy is punctuated with distinctive flavors, so too is their cuisine punctuated with onions and any of a broad spectrum of peppers. If you are an Aries, try experimenting more widely with paprika. You'll be pleasantly surprised. You might also try cooking with beer, but use only a good full-flavored English or English-style ale where the flavor of the hops is well pronounced.

If you are an Aries of the First Decan, and you are intending to come into harmony with another person, don't be shy, use applicable robust spices, such as Chili Pepper, Curry, Garlic, Horseradish, Mustard or Cloves to flavor the dishes of her or his primary sign.

If you are an Aries of the Second Decan, and you are intending to come into harmony with another person, use more subtle flavorings. You may be surprised with the results if you start with a nice cup of Chamomile tea. In the meal, use Rosemary, Saffron and Sesame to flavor the dishes of her or his primary sign.

If you are an Aries of the Third Decan, and you are intending to come into harmony with another person, use Anise, Sage and Cloves for the main meal, and choose from the likes of Maple, Nutmeg, Licorice or Spearmint with your dessert. A simple bowl of Vanilla Ice cream is also often effective. Cardamom, used in the cuisine of India, is also one of your spices. You may be surprised with the results of a nice cup of Sassafras tea.

## ARIES

*Fruits*
Grapefruit, Watermelon

*Vegetables*
Carrots, Hops, Onions, Peppers,
Pimentos, Radishes, Shallots

*Herbs & Spices*

First Decan—March 21 through 30:
Allspice, Basil, Chili Pepper, Coriander,
Cumin, Curry, Garlic, Ginger, Horse-
radish, Mustard, Pepper, Peppermint,
Anise, Cloves, Maple, Nutmeg, Sage,
Sarsaparilla, Sassafras

Second Decan—March 31 through
April 9: Bay leaves, Chamomile,
Chicory, Cinnamon, Citron, Ginseng,
Rosemary, Saffron, Sesame

Third Decan—April 10 through 19:
Anise, Cloves, Maple, Nutmeg, Sage,
Sarsaparilla, Sassafras, Cardamom,
Licorice, Spearmint, Thyme, Vanilla

# CREAM OF ONION SOUP

2 finely minced onions
4 cups milk
¼ teaspoon salt
3 tablespoons butter or margarine
1 tablespoon flour
  pepper

Heat but do not brown the butter. Heat the minced onions in the butter. Cover and cook for 5 minutes so that it steams but does not brown. Stir in the flour. Add the cream, salt and pepper. Cook 10 minutes. Pass grated Parmesan cheese when soup is served. Serves 4.

# STUFFED PEPPERS

4 large green peppers
½ cup uncooked rice
4 ounces broiled lamb
1 small onion or 2 thin slices garlic
¼ cup water
  salt and pepper

Cut about 1 inch off the point end of the peppers. Carefully remove all seeds from the inside. Boil rice by sprinkling it into 2 quarts of boiling salted water. Allow the rice to boil until quite tender and no hardness remains in the center. Then pour the rice into a large wire strainer and run plenty of cold water through it. This will wash out the excessive starch. Now cut the lamb into very small pieces and mix with the rice. Season and stuff each pepper with the mixture. Place the stuffed peppers in a pie pan and bake at 375° F for about 30 minutes. Prepare Tomato Sauce (recipe on page 61). To serve, place a stuffed pepper on each plate. Serves 4.

# GLAZED ONIONS

4 cups small white onions
2 tablespoons butter or
   margarine
2 teaspoons powdered
   sugar
¼ cup water

Peel the onions. Cook 20 minutes in boiling water. Drain. Place the butter in a saucepan. Melt. Add the onions with the powdered sugar. Shake occasionally until the butter has been absorbed and the onions are golden brown. Add the water. Cook until the water is absorbed. Serves 6.

# FROZEN CHEESE WITH GRAPEFRUIT

## SALAD

2 packages cream cheese
1 cup grapefruit juice
¼ cup powdered sugar
½ teaspoon paprika
1 tablespoon gelatine
3 tablespoon cold water
1 cup whipped cream
1 peeled and sliced fresh
   grapefruit

## DRESSING

½ cup olive oil
¼ cup grapefruit juice
1 teaspoon lemon juice
½ teaspoon salt
½ teaspoon paprika

Mash the cream cheese and blend with the grapefruit juice and sugar. Add this to the cheese gradually and add the paprika. Dissolve the gelatine in the cold water. Melt over hot water. Add the whipped cream and the melted gelatine to cheese. Place in a tray of the refrigerator and chill for 2 hours. Turn out on a decorative plate. Surround with fruit. Serve with French dressing made of the olive oil, grapefruit juice, lemon juice, salt and paprika. Beat this until creamy. Serves 6.

# INDIAN CURRY

1   small apple
1   cup raisins
2   tablespoons chopped
    onion
2   tablespoons butter or
    margarine
2   teaspoons curry powder
3   cloves or ¹⁄₁₆ teaspoon
    powdered cloves
1   teaspoon lemon juice
1   teaspoon cardamom if
    astrologically
    appropriate
    Rice (recipe below)
    broiled lamb, mutton
    or goat

Peel and cut up the apple and onion and put them into a frying pan with the butter. Brown, then squash into a paste and add curry powder, raisins, cloves and lemon juice and allow to slowly simmer for 10 minutes. Your curry mixture is now ready. Where you have a gravy, add water from the cooked rice to make 3 cups of liquid, then add the curry mixture. Serve by making wall of Rice (recipe below)

all around the dish and placing the broiled meat in the center, then pour over the gravy. For Curried Sausages bake the sausages in the oven, or fry if you prefer, then place 2 tablespoons of the hot sausage fat in a saucepan and mix in 1 tablespoon of flour, add 1 cup of boiling water from the rice, stir and add curry mix and sausages and allow to simmer for 15 to 20 minutes. Serves 6.

## TO COOK RICE:

Use plenty of salted water when cooking rice. I use about 2 quarts of water to 1 cup of rice. Have the water boiling. Wash and pick over the rice, then sprinkle it into the boiling water (if you grease the top 3 or 4 inches of the inside of the kettle the water will not boil over on top of the stove). Allow the rice to boil until quite tender, with no hardness in the grains; then pour it into a large wire strainer and thoroughly wash by pouring plenty of cold water over it, after which the rice should be reheated by placing in a slow oven with a cloth over the top, or you can stand the strainer with the rice over the opening of the bottom pot of a double boiler (the water must not touch the rice). Let the water boil so that the steam filters through the rice. Use a fork to lightly lift rice and loosen it up in the strainer. (Instant rice may be substituted.)

# ENGLISH MUTTON CHOPS

4 *2-inch thick mutton or lamb chops*
*astrologically appropriate herbs and spices*
4 *large potatoes*
*butter or margarine*
*paprika*

Wash and bake the potatoes. Broil the chops 20 minutes. Turn them often, sprinkling with the herbs and spices after turning. Serve with the potatoes which have been split open and pieces of butter inserted. Dust the potatoes with paprika. Surround the chops with sliced cooked carrots and sautéed onion rings. Serves 4.

# LAMB STEW

4 *lamb steaks or lamb chops*
2 *tablespoons butter or margarine*
1 *sliced onion*
1 *cup minced celery*
1 *cup minced carrots*
1 *tablespoon flour*
*salt and pepper*
2 *cups water*

Heat the butter in a frying pan. When butter is melted, add the celery, carrots and onion. Cook 2 minutes. Stir in the flour and add the water. Salt and pepper to taste. When thickened transfer to a saucepan. Cut the meat into small pieces. Save the bones for soup stock. Dust the meat with flour. Sauté the meat in butter and place on top of the vegetables. Cover and cook slowly for 25 minutes. Add more water if it cooks away. Pork, veal or beef may be used instead of lamb. Any meat left over from a roast will serve. Serves 4.

# BAYANDI ARIES

1 eggplant
1½ pounds stewing lamb
½ cup flour
1 20-ounce can tomatoes
1 cut up medium onion
4 tablespoons butter or
   margarine
1 cup water
   salt and pepper

Wash the eggplant and bake whole, with the skin on, at 375° F until quite soft when tested with a fork. While the eggplant is baking, stew the lamb. Cut it into pieces about 1 inch square; sift flour over the lamb and press flour into it. Put 2 tablespoons of butter into frying pan and when sizzling hot add the lamb and brown on all sides; add onion when lamb is nearly browned. When brown, add the water and tomatoes. Add salt and pepper to taste. Cover the pan and simmer for about 45 minutes, or until quite tender. This should now have a heavy tomato gravy.

When the eggplant is baked soft, remove from oven, peel and mash thoroughly (use a ricer). Season with salt and pepper, adding 2 tablespoons of butter and place in a saucepan over low heat as you mix in the seasonings and butter.

Serve the lamb stew on top of the mashed eggplant. Serves 4.

# ROAST LAMB

1   lamb roast (allow ½
    pound per serving)
¾   cup sifted flour
1   small onion or
    clove garlic
    salt and pepper

Wash meat and place in roasting pan. Then sift flour all over it. Some of the sifted flour will go into the baking pan, but that will dissolve when you add the water. Sprinkle well with salt and pepper and then pour cold water into the baking pan to the depth of about 1 inch. On top of the roast place slices of onion, or if you like a slight taste of garlic. Then do this: With a knife cut 5 or 6 deep holes in the top of the roast and push one very small piece of garlic, the size of a pin, into each hole.

Place the roast in the center of the oven and bake at 450° F for 30 minutes and then reduce heat to 325° F for balance of time. (Allow at least 30 minutes per pound.) Do not baste the roast for the first half hour, but after that baste it about every 15 minutes. Have a kettle of water boiling on the stove and in case the water boils away in the roast, pour in a little boiling water. During the last half hour the roast is cooking, turn it over and let the other side brown and then turn it back again 5 minutes before you take it out of the oven. The turning of the roast will help to color the gravy and soften up the meat. You will also find when your roast is ready to serve that you have plenty of rich gravy already made.

# TAURUS

## April 20 through May 19

| Ruling Element | Ruling Planet | Nouriture |
|:---:|:---:|:---:|
| **Earth** | **Venus** | **Beef** |

As a Taurus, you are strong and very down to earth. Unless you have chosen to lead a vegetarian life, your choices for a main dish revolve around beef. You may enjoy a good hamburger, and since tomatoes are yours, you probably enjoy that burger with a big slice of beefsteak tomato. Even the bun is made from grains associated with your sign. As a Taurus, you may also choose from a variety of other beef dishes.

Because your sign is ruled by mother Venus, you may also feel harmonious with a wide variety of fruits and berries. These may be prepared in pies or tarts as well as being eaten fresh from the tree or vine. If you are a Taurus, try experimenting more widely with Avocados.

You are generous and like to share. As such, you will be pleased to prepare dishes for your friends that center on beef, or the nouriture associated with their sign, but spiced with the flavorings of your Decan.

If you are a Taurus of the First Decan, and you are intending to come into harmony with another person, use strong spices such as Chili Pepper, Curry, Garlic, Horseradish, and Mustard or the distinctive accents of Fennel or Mint to flavor the dishes of her or his primary sign.

If you are a Taurus of the Second Decan, and you are intending to come into harmony with another person, you should focus on such flavorings as Mint, Peppermint, and Wintergreen. You may also use Lemon flavoring, especially if your friend is a Cancer.

If you are a Taurus of the Third Decan, you are the member of a very exclusive club. You are blessed as having been born during one of the four weeks of the year for which Tamarind and Tarragon are the only spices. Take them. May they serve you well.

*Fruits*
Apples, Avocados, Bananas, Blackberries, Cherries, Huckleberries, Peaches, Pears, Persimmons, Plums, Raspberries, Rhubarb, Strawberries

*Vegetables*
Peas, Spinach, Tomatoes (listed as a vegetable, as it is used as such in contemporary cooking)

*Grains*
Barley, Corn, Oats, Rye, Wheat

*Herbs & Spices*

First Decan—April 20 through 28:
Bittersweet, Caraway, Clover, Dill, Fennel, Mint, Parsley, Peppermint, Allspice, Basil, Chili Pepper, Coriander, Cumin, Curry, Garlic, Ginger, Horseradish, Mustard, Pepper, Peppermint

Second Decan—April 29 through May 9:
Bittersweet, Caraway, Clover, Dill, Fennel, Mint, Parsley, Peppermint, Wintergreen

Third Decan—May 10 through 19:
Tamarind, Tarragon

# CREAM OF SPINACH SOUP

2 cups water
1 cup shredded spinach
2 thin slices onion
2 cups milk
¼ teaspoon salt
  pepper
4 thin slices cheese

Heat water. When boiling add the shredded spinach and slices of onion. Boil 5 minutes. Add the milk and the salt. Dust with pepper. Heat and serve. For variety this soup may be served in small casseroles. Lay a thin slice of cheese on the top of each portion and melt the cheese slightly in the oven. Serves 4.

# AVOCADO AND GROUND BEEF SALAD

1 cup cooked
  ground beef
½ cup celery
½ cup orange cubes
½ cup French Dressing
  (recipe on page 36)
2 tablespoons salsa
4 ripe avocados
  large green olives

Mix the ground beef, celery and orange cubes. Marinate in the French Dressing (recipe on page 36) with the salsa added. Cut the pears in half, remove the seeds and peel them. Fill the halves with ground beef. Mask the meat with mayonnaise. Serve on crisp lettuce. Remove seeds from large green olives and use to garnish salad. Serves 6.

# JELLIED TOMATO BOUILLON

1  20-ounce can tomatoes
   or 6 fresh tomatoes
2  tablespoons granulated
   gelatin
¼  cup cold water
½  cup boiling water
1  small finely chopped
   onion
½  teaspoon celery salt or
   some chopped tops of
   celery stalks
2  bay leaves
1/16 teaspoon powdered
   cloves
   salt and pepper
   finely chopped parsley

Cook very slowly for 20 to 25 minutes the tomatoes, onions, celery salt or tops, bay leaves, cloves and salt and pepper to taste. When tomatoes have been cooking 15 minutes, soak gelatin in cold water for 5 minutes, then dissolve in ½ cup of boiling water. Then strain the tomato mixture through a wire sieve and press all juice out. Add the gelatine mixture and stir to mix thoroughly. Allow to cool. When cold place in refrigerator or ice box until it jells solid. Serve in bouillon cups, first cutting the jellied tomato bouillon into small pieces or break up fine with a fork. Garnish it with some finely chopped parsley. Serves 4.

*Note:* The veal knuckle, or calf's foot, is used to jell the soup. The soup can be made quickly by using canned bouillon and tomato juice, 1 can of bouillon to ¼ can of tomato juice, and using granulated gelatine, but the soup will not be nearly as good, as the gelatine will make a jelly that is too stiff. The veal knuckle, or calf's foot, is the correct thing to use and either of them will give you a jellied soup that is soft and smooth and much more delicious than that made from canned soup, tomatoes and gelatine.

# SWEET POTATOES WITH APPLES

3 sweet potatoes
1 cup water
1 cup brown sugar
3 sliced cooking apples
  (such as Granny Smiths
  or Pippins)
½ teaspoon salt
¼ teaspoon nutmeg
3 tablespoons butter or
  margarine

Peel and cut the potatoes into slices. Boil 10 minutes. Boil 1 cup water with the sugar. Add the apples, salt and nutmeg. Cook 8 minutes. Stir in the butter. Drain the potatoes. Arrange them in a baking dish. Begin with a layer of potatoes, then a layer of apples and continue until dish is filled. Pour the liquid over them. Bake at 375° F for 10 minutes. Serves 4.

# CREAMY CORN PUDDING

2½ cups fresh or frozen
   (thawed) corn
2 cups milk
3 eggs
1 teaspoon salt
¼ teaspoon white pepper

Place the corn in a deep buttered baking dish. Separate the eggs. Add the unbeaten egg yolks and stir in well. Then add the milk, salt, and pepper and stir to thoroughly mix the egg yolks with the other ingredients. Beat white of eggs until stiff, so that the beaten egg stands up in a point when the rotary egg beater is lifted out. Empty the beaten egg white onto the milk mixture and cut and fold it in by cutting down through the beaten white, bringing spoon along the bottom, and up and over the egg white, and cutting down through it again. Continue to cut and fold (as this is called) until the egg white is mixed in smoothly, and no pieces of beaten egg white remain floating. Place in center of a moderate oven and bake at 375° F for 1 hour. Serves 6.

# POT OF BEEF TAURUS

3 pounds pot roast
2 tablespoons salt
1 teaspoon black pepper
1 bundle carrots
1 bundle white turnips
4 leeks (more if preferred)
  few sprigs of parsley
1 cup fresh peas

Place beef in large kettle and add four quarts of cold water. Bring to a boil and skim the top of the water. Continue to skim off any scum until it ceases to form. Then add 2 tablespoons of salt and 1 teaspoon of black pepper. Prepare the leeks by taking off the outside layer and cutting off about ⅔ of the length of green, leaving the remainder of leeks whole. Chop up the rest of the green sections. Clean and cut up the other vegetables. Add the leeks and all the vegetables except the peas. Add the parsley and allow the whole to slowly simmer for 1¾ hours. Add the peas and continue to simmer for another 15 minutes. Then take the beef out and allow it to chill. (The roast can be eaten hot if preferred.) You will notice that the beef will swell up to more than twice the size that it was in the raw state.

When you take the meat out of the soup, remove the soup pot from the heat and reheat the soup when you are ready to serve the meat. The beef is eaten cold, with hot vegetables, including the leeks. Some of the vegetables can be cut up small and left in the soup and others left in larger pieces and served with the meat course. Serves 8.

# MEAT LOAF

1 pound ground lean round steak (½ pound ground pork may be substituted for ½ pound of the beef)
½ 20 ounce can tomatoes
1 teaspoon salt
½ teaspoon celery salt
½ teaspoon onion salt
¼ teaspoon dry mustard
½ teaspoon thyme
½ teaspoon ground sage
¼ teaspoon pepper
  other astrologically appropriate herbs and spices
1 teaspoon Worcestershire sauce
¾ cup bread crumbs
2 tablespoons flour
1 cup cold water

In a bowl put the meat, tomatoes and seasonings. Mix thoroughly with a large spoon. Add just enough bread crumbs to hold the meat together, form into a large egg shaped loaf and place in a small baking pan. Do not press it into a loaf pan but a loaf pan may be used to bake it in provided it is large enough to leave air space all around the meat loaf. A pie or round cake pan may also be used. *Let it stand in the refrigerator at least 1 hour* to allow the seasonings to be absorbed by the meat. Then pour water into the pan to the depth of ½ inch and place in a 400° F oven. Bake for 1 hour, basting occasionally. Reduce heat to 350° F during the last half hour. Remove meat loaf to hot plate and keep in a warm place while making the gravy. (Letting the meat stand for 15 minutes makes it much easier to slice.)

To make the gravy, place the pan over medium heat and sift the flour in over the fat and browned meat juices and mix well with a fork, stirring constantly. Then gradually add 1 cup of cold water, stirring until the mixture boils. Rub the fork over the browned juices until dissolved into the gravy. These juices will color and flavor it. Season the gravy with salt to taste. Serves 4.

# STROGANOFF TAURUS

1½ pounds lean beef (Any cut of beef can be used, but, of course, the better the beef, the better the Stroganoff. Top round steak is very good.)
½ pound fresh or 1 can mushrooms
3 tablespoons butter or margarine
1 cup sour cream
1 tablespoon flour
salt and paprika

Cut the beef across the grain. If you cut with the grain the meat will be stringy and tough, whereas if you cut across the grain, the meat will be tender. First stretch the meat to see which way the grain runs and then cut across the grain. Cut the beef into little pieces about 1 inch long and about half the width of a pencil. Place 2 tablespoons butter into a frying pan and when hot add the beef. Cover and simmer gently for 15 minutes, turning the meat over occasionally. Cut the mushrooms into fairly small pieces, add and cook with the beef for 10 minutes. If the pan becomes dry, add a little butter.

Pour the meat and mushrooms in the top part of a double boiler. Put 1 tablespoon of butter in the frying pan, melt and stir in the flour. Then add the sour cream. (Sweet cream or Cream Sauce can be used, but does not compare with sour cream, which is always used by Russians.) If cream mixture is too thick, add a little milk. Place pan over heat and stir with a fork to mix the meat juices of the pan with the cream mixture. Then pour this into the beef and mushrooms in the double boiler and cook for 5 or 10 minutes. Season to taste. Serve on large biscuits slit in half and toasted on the cut side only. The Russians usually serve this with Julienne Potatoes. Serves 4.

*Note:* For more gravy, add a little extra sweet cream or milk.

*To reheat:* This dish reheats perfectly and can be kept in the refrigerator, then reheated by placing in saucepan over low heat and adding a little sweet cream. Stir until it boils, then serve. For dinner parties, this can be prepared the day before.

# GEMINI

## May 20 through June 20

| *Ruling Element* | *Ruling Planet* | *Nouriture* |
|:---:|:---:|:---:|
| **Air** | **Mercury** | **Fowl** |

As a Gemini, you are versatile and accommodating, embodying a duality that makes you capable of understanding a wide spectrum of human nature, and enjoying a wide variety of foods. As such, I have chosen to focus primarily on fruits and vegetables that are most strongly associated with you, although you may choose from virtually the entire cornucopia.

You are multifaceted, but basically your nature is of the air. As such, unless you have chosen to lead a vegetarian life, your choices for a primary main dish include all Fowl: Chicken, Duck, Turkey, Squab, Game Hen, or any of the Wild Fowl such as Pheasant, Quail or Grouse.

Conversely, you are one of three signs for whom nuts are an essential food. If anyone calls you nutty, don't take it as insult, just wink knowingly and go back to preparing the dressing for your Turkey.

Owing to the complex nature of Gemini's multifaceted personality, is there any wonder that the deliciously intricate Pomegranate is one of your principal fruits?

If you are a Gemini of the First Decan, and you are intending to come into harmony with another person, You should focus on the intensity of sage and cloves to flavor the dishes of her or his primary sign. Maple, Nutmeg, Licorice or Spearmint will be perfect with your dessert. A simple bowl of Vanilla Ice cream is also often effective. You may be surprised with the results of a nice cup of Sassafras tea.

If you are a Gemini of the Second Decan, and you are intending to come into harmony with another person, your pallet of spices to please

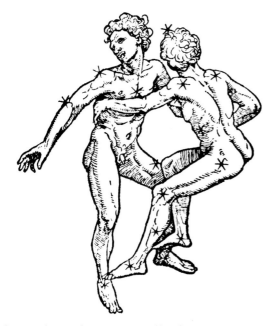

*Fruits*
Apricots, Pomegranates

*Vegetables*
Beans, Broccoli, Cauliflower, Celery

*Nuts*
Almonds, Brazil Nuts, Filberts, Pecans, Pistachios

*Herbs & Spices*

First Decan—May 20 through 29:
Cardamom, Licorice, Spearmint, Thyme, Vanilla, Anise, Cloves, Maple, Nutmeg, Sage, Sarsaparilla, Sassafras

Second Decan—May 30 through June 7:
Cardamom, Licorice, Sage, Spearmint, Thyme, Vanilla

Third Decan—June 8 through 20:
Bay leaves, Chamomile, Chicory, Cinnamon, Citron, Ginseng, Rosemary, Saffron, Sesame

her or his palate is virtually the same as your neighbor in Gemini's First Decan. As with them, Cardamom, used in the cuisine of India, is also one of your spices. However, that cup of Sassafras tea is entirely optional.

If you are a Gemini of the Third Decan, and you are intending to come into harmony with another person, your spices are the distinct flavors of Cinnamon, Citron, Ginseng, Rosemary and Saffron. For you, it is Chamomile tea.

# CREAM OF CELERY SOUP

2 cups thinly sliced celery
3 cups water
2 cups milk
¼ teaspoon salt
pepper
2 tablespoons butter or margarine
paprika
4 sprigs parsley

Slice celery into very thin slices. Cook in boiling water for 15 minutes. Add the milk and salt. Dust with pepper. When hot add butter. Dust each serving with paprika and add a sprig of parsley. Leftover cooked celery may be utilized for this soup. Serves 4.

# CHICKEN SALAD

3 cups diced chicken
½ cup sliced ripe stuffed olives
1 cup finely chopped celery
½ cup pineapple in thin slices
capers
French Dressing (recipe on page 36)
mayonnaise
sliced almonds

Mix the chicken meat with the celery. Add the pineapple which has been cut into thin, finger-like slices. Add the olives. Let this marinate in French Dressing (recipe on page 36) in the refrigerator for 1 hour. Drain. Arrange in salad bowl. Mask with mayonnaise. Decorate with capers, sliced ripe olives and sliced almonds. Serves 6.

# CAULIFLOWER WITH LEMON SAUCE

1   head cauliflower
2   eggs
    salt and pepper
    juice of 1 lemon
1   cup hot milk
2   cups chopped almonds
    or pecans
1   tablespoon minced parsley

Cut the cauliflower into small pieces. Drop into boiling salted water. Cook 15 minutes. Serve with lemon sauce. To prepare sauce: Beat the eggs with salt, pepper and lemon juice. Add the hot milk. Cook in a double boiler until it thickens. Add the chopped almonds or pecans. Add the parsley. The same amount of minced chives or capers may be used if appropriate. Serves 4.

# CACCIATORA GEMINI

1   roasting chicken
3   red or green peppers
4   medium onions
6   sliced apricots or
    canned, drained
    apricots
¾   cup olive oil
1   can tomatoes
3   cloves garlic
    salt and pepper

Place half the olive oil into a frying pan which has a lid or use a baking pan with cover. Wash the chicken and cut up into small pieces. Sprinkle salt and pepper over chicken and put into the hot olive oil. Cover and simmer gently 1½ hours or until tender.

One half hour before chicken is done cut onions into slices and place into another frying pan with the rest of the olive oil. Cook slowly for about 15 minutes. At the same time place the tomatoes in a pot. Season to taste, add the garlic and simmer for 30 minutes.

While the onions are cooking, remove seeds from peppers and cut into strips about 1 inch wide. Add the peppers and apricots to the onions after the onions have cooked 15 minutes and simmer for 10 minutes. Then add the onions and peppers to the chicken and simmer for 10 more minutes. Then add the tomatoes, which should be cooked into a sauce and serve. Serves 4.

# ROAST GOOSE WITH POTATO STUFFING

1   egg
1   roasting goose (allow ½
    pound per serving)
5   large potatoes
2   tablespoons chopped
    nuts (almonds, brazil
    nuts, filberts, pecans
    and/or pistachios)
1   medium onion
1   teaspoon caraway seed
    (if astrologically
    appropriate)
1   tablespoon chopped
    parsley
    other astrologically
    appropriate herbs and
    spices to taste
1   tablespoon melted
    butter or margarine

Wash potatoes and boil them with their skins on. When done, peel and mash, grating and adding the onion to the mashed potatoes; add the nuts and desired herbs, caraway seed, chopped parsley, melted butter and egg. Mix all together and season to taste with salt and pepper. Then stuff the goose with this mixture. Sew the goose up carefully where the stuffing was put in, using an in-and-over lacing stitch. It is important to sew up the opening in the goose in order that the liquid does not run in when the goose is being basted. The goose should be thoroughly washed before being stuffed. Also remove some of the fat. Before placing the goose in the roasting pan put the roasting pan over the heat and place in it all the goose fat that you removed. When this is melted place the goose in the pan and with a large spoon baste the melted fat over the goose. Now sift some flour all over the goose; turn it over and sift flour on other side; then sprinkle well with salt and pepper and bake at 450° F for 30 minutes. Then reduce heat to 350° F and roast 20 minutes to the pound. Be sure to baste every 15 minutes.

Make a delicious gravy when the goose is finished roasting. Remove the goose from the roasting pan to a large platter. Then pour the hot grease from the roasting pan into a crock, leaving only 2 tablespoonfuls in the pan. Into these 2 tablespoons of hot fat sift 3 tablespoons of flour, stirring vigorously with a fork, until the mixture is browned. The flour must be completely mixed with the hot grease so that there are no lumps. Then pour in 3 cups of water. Place roasting pan over moderate heat and stir constantly until the gravy thickens. Stir thoroughly in order to mix in the browned juices which have so-lidified on the bottom of the roasting pan. This will color and flavor the gravy. Salt and pepper the gravy to taste.

# CHICKEN JAMBALAYA

| | |
|---|---|
| 2 | 2½ pound chickens |
| | salt and pepper to taste |
| ⅓ | cup butter or margarine |
| 2 | tablespoons chopped onion |
| 2 | cups rice |
| | pinch of saffron |
| 1 | bay leaf |
| 8 | sprigs fresh parsley |
| 1 | sprig thyme |
| 1½ | quarts chicken broth (6 cups) |
| | minced parsley |

Use a Dutch oven in preparing this dish. Clean, wash and cut up the chickens into serving pieces as for stew. Season to taste with salt and pepper and brown nicely over moderate heat in the butter, turning the pieces frequently. When golden brown, lift out the chicken and keep hot by placing on a plate and covering with aluminum foil. Lightly brown the onion in the remaining butter in the pan. Then stir in the well-washed and drained rice, adding more butter if needed so that each grain will be moistened by the butter and stirring in the saffron, mixing well. Bundle together the bay leaf, fresh parsley and thyme, all tied together with white kitchen thread. Add to the rice and cook for 5 minutes, stirring occasionally. Arrange the chicken over the rice and gently pour the chicken broth over everything. Bring to a rapid boil, stir and cover tightly. Place the pan in the oven and bake at 375° to 400° F for about 25 to 30 minutes, or until the rice has absorbed all the stock or liquid. Discard the bundled spices and arrange the rice on a heated platter, with the chicken on top. Dust with minced parsley. Serve immediately. Serves 4.

# CHICKEN & DUMPLINGS

1 cut up roasting chicken
(fricassee chicken can
be used if desired)
¾ cup sifted flour
2 tablespoons butter or
margarine
1 tablespoon salt
½ teaspoon pepper
1 small white onion
boiling water
Dumplings (recipe
follows)

You can use either a roasting or a fricassee chicken, but of course the roasting chicken will be better and will cook quicker. I generally use a 4 or 5 pound chicken. Clean the chicken, cut up and wash thoroughly in cold water. Reserve the extra fat. Sift ¾ cup of flour into a large bowl. Place pieces of chicken into the flour and press in as much flour as it will take up. Before you start to cook the chicken, chop the onion very fine. Put a kettle of water on the stove to boil. Now you have everything ready to cook the chicken.

Into a large pot put any chicken fat from the chicken. Put the pot over the heat and melt the chicken fat, adding the 1 tablespoon butter. Into this sizzling fat place the pieces of floured chicken and brown both sides of each piece. Put in new pieces of chicken as the first are browned, lifting the browned pieces to a plate as the other pieces are being browned. If the pot becomes too dry add more butter as necessary. When all the chicken is brown add the onion and let that slightly brown. Return chicken to pot and add enough boiling water to just cover the chicken, seasoning with the salt and black pepper. Allow this to just simmer, covering the pot with the lid. Simmer a roasting chicken for 2 hours. Allow a fricassee chicken to simmer longer. Also, with a fricassee chicken you may have to add a little boiling water from time to time, in case the gravy boils down. Serve with Dumplings (recipe follows). Serves 4.

## DUMPLING RECIPE

1½   cups sifted flour
1½   teaspoons salt
4   teaspoons baking
      powder
⅔   cup milk (no more)

Sift together flour, baking powder and salt and stir to thoroughly mix. Add milk slowly and mix into a heavy wet dough. Take heaping teaspoons of dumpling dough and carefully float on top of chicken and gravy. The gravy should be heavy. If gravy is very thin, place dumplings on top of chicken. Place lid on pot and cook 15 minutes.

# CASSEROLE OF CHICKEN

2   tender 3 pound
      chickens
      salt and pepper
4   tablespoons flour
2   slices onion
½   pound sliced
      mushrooms
1   thin slice lemon peel
4   tablespoons butter or
      margarine
3   cups water
4   tablespoons cooking
      wine or juice of
      1 orange

Either a glass or earthenware casserole may be used. Heat the casserole. Cut the chickens into pieces for serving. Dust with flour, salt and pepper. Brown the chicken in hot butter in a frying pan. Lay the meat in the hot casserole. Cook the onion, mushrooms and lemon peel in frying pan. Add butter and stir in the flour. Add water and wine or orange juice. Salt and pepper to taste. When this has thickened pour it over the chicken in the casserole. Place in a 400° F oven. When the liquid in the casserole is bubbling reduce heat to 300° F and cook for 3 hours. Longer cooking will not harm this dish if it is cooked slowly. Serves 4.

# CANCER

## June 21 through July 22

| Ruling Element | Ruling Planet | Nouriture |
|---|---|---|
| **Water** | **Moon** | **Crab** |

As a Cancer, you are as traditional and home-loving as you are changeable and adventurous. Your sign is the Crab, and there is little wonder that, unless you have chosen to lead a vegetarian life, or you have an allergy to shellfish, your main dish is crab. This may include the soft-shelled Chesapeake Bay variety, the Northwest's ubiquitous Red Rock, the classic Dungeness or the mighty Alaska King Crab. The ersatz "crab" that is made from tinted fish should be avoided in all but rare occasions.

As befits the down home, back to basics nature of the Cancer, your vegetables are also very down to Earth, and include Potatoes, Turnips and Gourds as well as Cabbage and Lettuce. Your fruits, however, include the lofty Coconut.

If you are a Cancer of the First Decan, and you are intending to come into harmony with another person, use the fresh flavors of Wintergreen, Lemon peel, Licorice, Spearmint and Vanilla to add spice to their favorite dishes.

If you are a Cancer of the Second Decan, and you are intending to come into harmony with another person, you may choose from Allspice, Basil, Coriander, Cumin, Curry, Garlic, Ginger, Horseradish, Mustard, Pepper, Bittersweet, Caraway, Clover, Dill, Fennel or Parsley to flavor the dishes of her or his primary sign.

If you are a Cancer of the Third Decan, and you are intending to come into harmony with another person, use Wintergreen, Lemon peel, Anise, Cloves, Maple, Nutmeg or Sage, a spectrum of choices similar to, but subtly different from, those of your sister Decans.

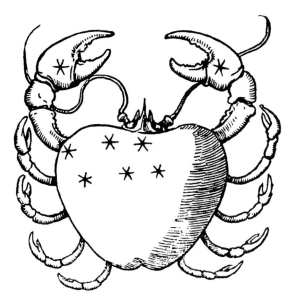

## CANCER

*Fruits*
Coconuts, Grapes, Lemons, Papayas

*Vegetables*
Cabbage, Cucumbers, Gourds, Lettuce, Potatoes, Turnips

*Herbs & Spices*

First Decan—June 21 through July 3:
Wintergreen, Lemon peel, Cardamom, Licorice, Sage, Spearmint, Thyme, Vanilla

Second Decan—July 4 through 14:
Allspice, Basil, Chili Pepper, Coriander, Cumin, Curry, Garlic, Ginger, Horse-radish, Mustard, Pepper, Peppermint, Bittersweet, Caraway, Clover, Dill, Fennel, Mint, Parsley, Peppermint

Third Decan—July 15 through 22:
Wintergreen, Lemon peel, Anise, Cloves, Maple, Nutmeg, Sage, Sarsaparilla, Sassafras

# CREAM OF POTATO SOUP

1 potato
1 small onion
2 cups boiling water
3 cups cream or milk
¼ teaspoon salt
2 tablespoons butter or
  margarine
  pepper
  finely minced parsley or
  mint leaves

Peel and slice the potato in very thin slices. Peel and slice the onion into thin slices. Cook rapidly in boiling water for 15 minutes. Add cream or milk and salt. Heat. Add butter. Dust with pepper. Sprinkle each portion with minced parsley. Fresh mint leaves, finely chopped, may be substituted for the parsley. Serves 4.

# CRAB AND POTATO SOUFFLÉ

3 eggs
2 cups mashed potatoes
  salt and pepper
1 tablespoon minced
  parsley
3 tablespoons cooked or
  canned crab meat

Separate the whites and yolks of the eggs. Beat the yolks into the mashed potatoes in a buttered baking dish. Add the salt and pepper, minced parsley and crab meat. Beat the egg whites until stiff. Fold into the potato mixture. Bake at 375° F for 25 minutes.

Another method is to place the dish in a pan of hot water in oven. Bake at 325° F for 60 minutes. Serve immediately. Serves 4.

# LEMON BUTTER POTATOES

4 potatoes
4 tablespoons butter or
   margarine
½ tablespoon lemon juice
1 teaspoon finely minced
   sweet red pepper
2 teaspoons minced
   parsley or chives

Peel potatoes. Cut them into balls with a vegetable cutter. Boil 20 minutes in salted water. Cream the butter. Add the lemon juice a little at a time. Add the finely minced sweet red pepper and minced parsley. Chives may be substituted for the parsley if appropriate. Serves 4.

# POTATO SOUP

6 medium peeled
   potatoes
2 small finely chopped
   onions
1 finely chopped carrot
4 cups milk
4 tablespoons butter or
   margarine
2 tablespoons flour
2 tablespoons finely
   chopped parsley
   salt and white pepper

Start potatoes in cold salted water. Cover and bring to a boil. Cook until done. Put butter in frying pan and place over heat. When a golden brown, add the finely chopped onion and carrot, and turn flame down under pan, or move on stove to where it will not cook too fast. Allow to slowly cook for 20 minutes; then sift in 2 tablespoons of flour and stir to thoroughly blend. When blended, add slowly about 1 cup milk, stirring while adding. Then pour the contents of the pan into a saucepan and add the rest of the milk. Mash 4 of the boiled potatoes (through a ricer is best) and cut the other 2 potatoes into very small pieces. Add all the potatoes to the other ingredients in the pot. Add the parsley and season to taste. Allow to simmer for a few minutes after the parsley and seasoning are added. Reheats perfectly. Serves 4.

# CANCERIAN POTATO SALAD

12  medium potatoes
2  medium onions
¼  pound almonds
½  cup finely chopped
    parsley
    French Dressing
    (recipe follows)
    Boiled Dressing
    (recipe follows)

Wash potatoes and boil them with their skins on, starting them in cold water with a lid on the pot and no salt in the water. While the potatoes are boiling, blanch the almonds by putting them in a cup and filling the cup with boiling water. In a few minutes the skins will remove easily. Cut these almonds into very fine slices. Now cut up the two onions very fine.

Potatoes should be boiled until they are thoroughly soft, and crack open. Then strain the water from them and remove skins, placing the potatoes in a large bowl. Break the potatoes up with a large spoon until like very coarse mashed potatoes; then make French Dressing (see below).

*Note:* This recipe makes a *large* bowl of potato salad.

## FRENCH DRESSING

1  teaspoon salt
1  teaspoon paprika
¼  teaspoon pepper,
    if desired
8  tablespoons olive oil
6  tablespoons vinegar

Place all ingredients in a small mason jar. Screw cap tight and shake well and the ingredients will become thick and well combined, or place ingredients in bowl and beat with rotary egg beater. Pour over the potatoes while still warm. Then make Boiled Dressing (recipe follows).

## BOILED DRESSING

3   tablespoons butter or
    margarine
1   teaspoon salt
1   teaspoon dry mustard
1   teaspoon paprika
3   egg yolks
1   cup hot milk
¼   cup hot vinegar

Place the butter in a bowl and stir until creamy. Add the salt, mustard and paprika; then separate 3 eggs and drop the 3 egg yolks into the butter mixture and stir around until thoroughly mixed. Heat 1 cup of milk in the top part of a double boiler; then pour the hot milk into the butter and egg mixture, stirring constantly while adding. Return this mixture to the double boiler and cook until thick. Then remove from heat and add a quarter of a cup of vinegar that has been heated. Stir this into the dressing.

Thoroughly mix in the potatoes, and at the same time add the finely sliced almonds, the finely chopped onion and parsley. Then stir the whole mixture together until thoroughly mixed. Chill and serve when wanted. (In the final mixing of the salad add a little salt if desired.)

# POTATO CAKES

2   cups mashed potatoes
1   egg
1   tablespoon flour
    salt and pepper to taste

Beat all ingredients together and form into cakes. Dip into flour and brown in butter. This mixture may be cooked in an omelet pan, browned on both sides and served in one big cake. This needs 8 minutes to brown. Serves 2.

# CREAMED POTATOES

6   potatoes
4   tablespoons flour
4   tablespoons butter or
    margarine
2   cups milk
½   teaspoon salt
    parsley

Peel and dice the potatoes. Drop into boiling water and cook 15 minutes. While they are cooking prepare the following sauce: Blend the flour and the butter. Put the milk in the top of a double boiler over low heat. Add the flour and butter and salt. Stir constantly, as this is easily burned. Join the parts of the double boiler and finish cooking over hot water until the potatoes are ready. Drain potatoes and add to the cream sauce. Sprinkle with minced parsley and appropriate herbs. Serves 4.

# POTTED RED CABBAGE

1   red cabbage
2   tablespoons butter or
    bacon fat
1   medium onion
2   chopped green apples
1   tablespoon lemon juice
1   tablespoon sugar
    salt and pepper

Cut cabbage up small and finely chop the onion. Place the butter or bacon fat into a pot. Put pot on moderate heat and when fat is hot add the onion. Then put in the finely chopped cabbage and cook for 30 minutes without water. Add the chopped apples, lemon juice and sugar. Salt and pepper to taste and allow this to cook for 30 minutes more, turning it over occasionally with a spoon. It is now ready to serve. Serves 4.

# CRAB CROQUETTES

2 cups crab meat or 1 cup crab meat and 1 cup cooked filet of sole
⅓ cup butter or margarine
½ cup flour
1 teaspoon salt
2 cups cold milk
fine dry bread crumbs or cracker crumbs
1 egg
1 teaspoon water
Cream Sauce (recipe on page 79)
minced parsley

Flake the meat and mix the crab with the filet of sole. Make a white sauce by blending the butter, flour and salt. Add to the milk. Stir over medium heat with a wire whisk, stirring constantly. When the ingredients are blended and thickened slightly cook for 10 minutes in a double boiler. Dust with pepper. Add the crab and fish. Spread in a shallow dish. Cool and place in the refrigerator to get thoroughly cold. Form into croquettes. Dip in dry sifted bread or cracker crumbs. Then in a beaten egg that has been diluted with 1 teaspoon of water. Dip again in the crumbs. Fry in a basket in deep, hot fat. The fat should be heated until it will brown a cube of bread in 1 minute (375° F). Decorate with parsley and lemon. Fresh green peas should accompany the croquettes. Cream Sauce (recipe on page 79) with minced parsley may be served with them. Serves 4.

# LEO

## July 23 through August 21

| Ruling Element | Ruling Planet | Nouriture |
|:---:|:---:|:---:|
| **Fire** | **Sun** | **Wild Game** |

As a Leo, you are powerful and expansive like the sun that rules your sign, or the lion which is its symbol. Indeed, like the lion, unless you have chosen to lead a vegetarian life, your nouriture is Wild Game. Because you are a fire sign, the full impact of your nouriture is achieved when the main dish is cooked over an open fire.

The fruits associated with Leo are tart and full-flavored, including Pineapples as well as three Citrus fruits: Limes, Oranges and Tangerines. Leo's vegetables are, not surprisingly, those which thrive in sunny climes: Okra, Olives and Squash.

Leo is also one of three signs with whom nuts are associated, but unlike the nuts shared in common by Gemini and Virgo, Cashews, Sunflower seeds and Walnuts are Leo's and Leo's alone.

While various herb teas are associated with the specific Decans of several signs, tea as a beverage belongs to Leo. The purest form, and the quintessential Leonine tea is Chinese Green tea, although for those born between August third through twelfth, Sassafras tea is extremely, and *uniquely*, important.

If you are a Leo of the First Decan, you are the member of a very exclusive club. You are blessed as having been born during one of the four weeks of the year for which Tamarind and Tarragon are the only spices. Take them. May they serve you well.

If you are a Leo of the Second Decan, and you are intending to come into harmony with another person, you may choose from Anise, Cloves, Maple, Nutmeg or Sage to flavor the dishes of her or his primary sign. A cup of Sassafras tea is an important ritual beverage for

## LEO

*Fruits*
Limes, Oranges, Pineapples, Tangerines

*Vegetables*
Okra, Olives, Squash

*Nuts*
Cashews, Sunflower seeds, Walnuts

*Grains*
Rice

*Herbs & Spices*

First Decan—July 23 through August 2:
Tamarind, Tarragon,

Second Decan—August 3 through 12:
Anise, Cloves, Maple, Nutmeg, Sage,
Sarsaparilla, Sassafras

Third Decan—August 13 through 21:
Allspice, Basil, Chili Pepper, Coriander,
Cumin, Curry, Garlic, Ginger, Horse-
radish, Mustard, Pepper, Peppermint

Second Decan Leos, and should two such persons get together, Sassafras tea verges on the
etherial.

    If you are a Leo of the Third Decan, and you
are intending to come into harmony with another person, use Allspice, Basil, Chili Pepper,
Coriander, Cumin, Curry, Garlic, Ginger,
Horseradish, Mustard, or Pepper to flavor the
food that you prepare for them, and use Peppermint to add that special sparkle to their lives
and to your relationship.

# WILD GAME CHILI

| | |
|---|---|
| 1 | pound ground or chopped venison, elk or buffalo |
| 1 | 20-ounce can red kidney beans |
| 1 | 20-ounce can tomatoes |
| 1 | small okra |
| 1½ | tablespoons chili powder |
| 1 | medium onion |
| 1 | large or 2 small cloves garlic |
| 1½ | teaspoons caraway seed |
| 1½ | teaspoons flour |
| 1½ | teaspoons black pepper |
| 1½ | teaspoons salt, or to taste |
| 2 | tablespoons butter or margarine |

Put 1 tablespoon of butter into a frying pan. When hot, add the meat and spread in pan. Brown well. Break it up, and turn it over to let it all brown; then put it into a large pot, which should first be greased with a little melted butter. Have moderate heat under the pot, and then add to the meat the red kidney beans, the tomatoes, the chili powder, salt, and black pepper. Then cut onion into small pieces; very finely chop and crush the garlic with a knife. Put a tablespoon of butter in the frying pan and fry the onion and garlic to a rich brown. While they are frying, chop the okra fine and add to pot with meat, etc.

When the onions and garlic are browned, add them also. Now put the caraway seed in a piece of clean white cloth, and hammer it to thoroughly crush. Sift the flour into a pie pan and sprinkle in the crushed caraway seed; place this over heat to brown, or brown it in a hot oven.

The meat mixture should cook slowly for at least 45 minutes or until meat is tender. Stir often to prevent it sticking and burning. Just before it is finished cooking, add the browned flour and caraway seed. Stir well to mix in and allow to cook for 3 or 4 minutes. Serves 4.

# AMBROSIA SALAD

1 can seedless grapes
4 oranges
6 slices pineapple
1 package cream cheese
1 cup Lemon Mayonnaise
  (recipe follows)
½ cup whipped cream
  lettuce

Drain the seedless grapes. Peel the oranges. Cut the fruit into squares, discarding the white, pithy portions. Dice the pineapple. Drain all the fruit well. For the dressing blend the cheese with Lemon Mayonnaise (see below) and add whipped cream. Put together just before serving. Serve in nests of chilled lettuce. Serves 6.

# LEMON MAYONNAISE

1 egg
1 teaspoon salt
4 teaspoons sugar
  juice of 1 lemon
2 cups olive oil
  whipped cream
  (optional)
  food coloring (optional)

Beat the egg for 2 minutes. Add salt, sugar and lemon juice. Beat this together. Add olive oil, 1 teaspoon at a time, beating between each addition. Beat until thick. Whipped cream may be added when using. The dressing can be colored pale rose or green with food coloring.

# RISOTTO AI FUNGHI

3 cans chicken con-
somme, or 8 cups broth
from a fricassee chicken
3 cans beef bouillon
2 large onions
3 fresh tomatoes, or
½ can tomatoes
2 cups Italian dried
mushrooms
6 ounces freshly grated
Parmesan cheese
½ cup butter or margarine
(¼ pound)
2 cups rice (Italian rice
preferably)
salt and pepper

Prepare mushrooms by pouring boiling water over them and allowing them to soak 3 to 4 hours, changing the water 2 or 3 times. After they have soaked, drain and chop into very small pieces. Place a large frying pan, or pot, over medium heat and put the butter in it. When melted put in the onions, which have been chopped fairly small. Allow to become golden, but not brown, turning the onions over occasionally. Then add the dry rice and turn over to mix thoroughly with the hot butter and onions. Cook for about 1 minute to thoroughly heat the rice, turning it over as it cooks to prevent sticking. Then add 2½ cups of broth, or 2 cans, 1 of chicken consommé and 1 of bouillon, and stir well. Then, with your hands, break up the tomatoes and add to the rice. Continue to add more broth as the rice absorbs it, so as to keep a layer of broth on top of the cooking rice, just covering it. Stir often to prevent sticking. If you run short of broth before the rice is thoroughly cooked, you may add boiling water. Be sure, however, not to add too much liquid just before the rice is finished cooking.

In the last period of cooking, just before the rice is to be served, it should be allowed to absorb all excess liquid. Five minutes before rice is ready, add the finely chopped mushrooms. A minute before serving, while still on the stove, sprinkle grated Parmesan cheese over the cooking rice and mix in well. Grated Parmesan cheese is also served in a separate dish and passed at the table. Serves 4.

# CASSEROLE OF SUMMER SQUASH

2  summer squash
1  tablespoon butter or margarine
4  tablespoons cream
2  tablespoons minced ham
   dry roasted sunflower seeds or cashews

Peel the summer squash. Cut in small pieces and cook 20 minutes in boiling salted water. Drain, mash and add the butter, cream and minced ham. Remove to utility dish. Sprinkle top with dry roasted sunflower seeds or cashews. Bake at 350° F until the top is brown. Serves 4.

# GULYAS LEO

2  pounds venison or other wild game
¾  cup flour
2  tablespoons butter or margarine
1  tablespoon paprika
½  tablespoon salt
1  small onion
1  small clove garlic
1  cup hot water

A pot with a cover is required. Cut veal into small pieces and roll the pieces in flour, pressing in as much flour as possible. Put the pot over moderate heat and add butter. When butter is sizzling hot add venison, salt and paprika. Stir until thoroughly browned, then add the hot water, finely minced onion and garlic.

Cover the saucepan with a lid and allow to cook very slowly until tender (about 45 minutes). No more water need be added as the 1 cup will give you enough gravy. The gravy will color and thicken itself while cooking. Serve over Spaetzle Leo (recipe on following page). Serves 4.

# Spaetzle Leo

1   cup sifted flour
1   egg
½   teaspoon salt
½   teaspoon baking
     powder
½   cup milk

Put all ingredients in a bowl and mix thoroughly with a tablespoon. Do not beat. Fill a large pot half full with water. When the water boils drop the dumpling dough into it, one tablespoon at a time. Cover the pot with a lid and allow to boil for 10 minutes. Then drain the water from the dumplings and serve with the goulash gravy.

# Sausages Leo

1   pound wild game
     sausages
1   fresh okra
1   can tomato sauce
2   cups cold water
6   medium onions or 2
     large Spanish onions
2   tablespoons butter or
     margarine
2   tablespoons sifted flour

Place sausages in roasting pan and bake at 450° F until brown. Drain off the fat from the pan. Slice and add okra, ½ can of tomato sauce and 1 cup of water. Stir. Return the pan to the oven. After you first put the sausages in the oven, start to prepare and cook the onions as follows: Slice the onions, not too thin; then halve or quarter the slices. Sauté in the butter slowly for about 10 to 12 minutes. When they are cooked and slightly browned, add them to the sausages. Then place 2 tablespoons of flour in frying pan and return the pan to the heat. Stir the flour around until it is a deep brown. Add the remaining tomato sauce and water. Stir this mixture thoroughly, bring to a boil and simmer for 2 or 3 minutes. Pour into the roasting pan with the sausages and okra and bake for 10 or 15 minutes more. Serves 6.

# BRAISED VENISON

| | |
|---|---|
| 4 | pounds venison chops or wild boar, if available |
| ¼ | pound salt pork |
| 1 | cup diced celery |
| 1 | cup diced carrots |
| 1 | cup diced turnips |
| 1 | cup sliced okra |
| 8 | small white onions, or more if desired |
| 2 | tablespoons flour |
| 1 | quart hot water |
| 1 | small clove garlic, if desired |
| 1 or 2 | bay leaves astrologically appropriate spices and herbs |

Cut the salt pork into small pieces and put at the bottom of pot or a large casserole pot with a tight cover. You can successfully braise only in a pot with a perfectly tight cover. Place pot over low heat and melt the salt pork. Add the diced vegetables. The meat should be first sprinkled with salt and pepper. Then sift flour over it and press in with the hand. Add the meat to the vegetables and salt pork. Cook for 15 to 20 minutes and then add the hot water and allow to simmer very slowly for 3 or 4 hours, or until the meat is tender. The meat should be basted and turned occasionally. If the water boils down, add fresh boiling water. There should be at least 2 cups of gravy when the meat is cooked. Serve by placing the meat on a hot serving platter and the vegetables around it. Serves 8.

# VIRGO

## August 22 through September 22

*Ruling Element*
**Earth**

*Ruling Planet*
**Mercury**

*Nouriture*
**Veal**

As a Virgo, you are introspective and deliberate with a keen ability to analyze situations. Unless you have chosen to lead a vegetarian life, your nouriture, which shares the initial letter of your sign, is Veal.

Owing to the complex nature of the Virgo personality, it is little wonder that the deliciously intricate Pomegranate is one of your principal fruits. The Apricot, close cousin to the Peach of Taurus and Libra, is also a Virgo fruit.

The vegetables associated with Virgo are Broccoli, Cauliflower and Celery, which you share with Gemini. Also, like Gemini, nuts such as Almonds, Brazil Nuts, Filberts, Pecans and Pistachios are an essential food.

If you are a Virgo of the First Decan, and you are intending to come into harmony with another person, you may choose from Bay leaves, Chicory, Cinnamon, Citron, Rosemary, Saffron or Sesame to flavor the food that you prepare for her or him.

A cup of Chamomile tea is a good start as well as a good finish to the meal that you share. A cup of Ginseng tea is very effective, especially when shared with a Second Decan Aries, a Third Decan Gemini, a Second Decan Scorpio, a Third Decan Sagittarius or a Third Decan Capricorn.

Virgo's Second and Third Decans are the only case in the entire Zodiac where two consecutive Decans of the same sign are served by the same group of spices. If you are a member of this unique club, Sage and Thyme may be used to accent a main dish, and Vanilla and Spearmint may find their way into a dessert. Cardamom, used in the cuisine of India, is also one of your spices.

# VIRGO

*Fruits*
Apricots, Pomegranates

*Vegetables*
Beans, Broccoli, Cauliflower, Celery

*Nuts*
Almonds, Brazil Nuts, Filberts, Pecans, Pistachios

*Herbs & Spices*

First Decan—August 22 through 31:
Bay leaves, Chamomile, Chicory, Cinnamon, Citron, Ginseng, Rosemary, Saffron, Sesame

Second Decan—September 1 through 11:
Cardamom, Licorice, Sage, Spearmint, Thyme, Vanilla

Third Decan—September 12 through 22:
Cardamom, Licorice, Sage, Spearmint, Thyme, Vanilla

# LIMA BEAN SOUP

1   can lima beans
3   cups soup stock
1   tablespoon butter or
    margarine
1   tablespoon flour
    salt and pepper
    croutons
    finely minced parsley
    sliced lemon
    paprika

Put lima beans through a sieve. Add them to the soup stock. Blend butter with flour. Add to the soup together with salt and pepper. Cook 5 minutes. Add croutons to each portion, sprinkle with minced parsley and serve with slices of lemon dusted with paprika. Serves 4.

# BAKED BEANS

4   cups white navy beans
½   teaspoon baking soda
    (if desired)
3   teaspoons salt
1   teaspoon dry mustard
4   tablespoons molasses or
    brown sugar (optional)
1   onion or small
    clove garlic
½   pound broiled and
    chopped veal
3   tablespoons butter or
    margarine

Soak beans overnight. Drain and cover with fresh cold water. Bring to the boiling point, then add soda and simmer slowly for 30 minutes. If no soda is used, simmer longer, until tender. Test by piercing with large needle. Drain, and pour half of the beans into a bean pot. Add the salt, mustard, onion and the molasses. Cut veal into small pieces and add. Then put in the other half of the beans and barely cover the whole with boiling water. Cover the bean pot and bake in a slow oven for 8 hours. The lid should be taken off the bean pot for the last hour of cooking. If the beans become dry, add a little more water. The baked beans may be prepared with or without molasses, peppers or brown sugar. Serves 8.

# VIRGO FRUIT SALAD

1 large ripe fresh
  pineapple
1 cup diced fresh apricot
½ cup halved and seeded
  grapes
½ cup diced celery
½ cup slightly broken
  pecan nuts
1 cup Mayonnaise Cream
  Dressing (recipe follows)
1 head lettuce

With a large, sharp knife, cut both ends of the pineapple off and keep the end with the leaves. Then carefully cut the pineapple fruit out by cutting around inside the pineapple shell, from one end, then cutting down and around inside the shell from the other end until the fruit is removed. Be careful not to break the pineapple shell as the salad is served in this. When the pineapple fruit is removed, cut in slices, remove the hard center and dice the pineapple fruit. Mix with it the diced apricot and celery, the halved and seeded grapes, and the broken pecan nuts. Place all these ingredients together in a bowl. Then mix in 1 cup of Mayonnaise Cream Dressing (see below). Chill in refrigerator. Serves 8.

## MAYONNAISE CREAM DRESSING

½ cup mayonnaise
½ cup whipping cream

Beat the whipping cream until stiff. Add the mayonnaise. Fold gently together. Chill.

# CAULIFLOWER AU GRATIN

1 cauliflower
1 tablespoon lemon juice
2 tablespoons butter or margarine
4 tablespoons flour
2 cups cold milk
½ cup grated cheese
crushed pecans

Wash the cauliflower. Remove the green leaves. Cut into florets. Soak in cold water with the lemon juice. Boil 20 minutes. While the cauliflower is boiling make the sauce: Blend the butter with the flour. Add the cold milk. Cook in a double boiler. Stir until blended and then stir occasionally. Add the grated cheese. Remove cauliflower to utility dish. Dress with the cream sauce. Sprinkle top with crushed pecans. Bake at 350° F about 10 minutes until the top is brown. Serves 4.

# VEAL GOULASH VIRGO

2 pounds leg of veal
4 tablespoons butter or margarine
2 small or 1 large tomato
3 or 4 large onions
1 cup chopped celery
½ of 2-ounce jar capers (use the capers and the liquid)
2 tablespoons real Hungarian paprika
1 cup sour cream
salt and pepper
water

First prepare the ingredients. Chop onions into fairly small pieces. Cut the veal into very small squares. Put the butter into a large saucepan, or a frying pan which has a close fitting lid and place saucepan over moderate heat. When butter is hot, put in the chopped onion and allow to cook until a golden brown color. Then add the veal, salt, pepper and paprika. Continue to cook until the meat browns. Keep turning the onion and meat over every few minutes to prevent burning. When brown add tomato and celery, cut up, and two tablespoons of water. Cover and cook slowly for 45 minutes, adding about one tablespoon of water from time to time as necessary. When all has cooked for 45 minutes, add the capers and sour cream and allow to cook for a few minutes, then serve with fine noodles. Serves 4.

# RAGOUT DE VEAU

3 pounds breast of veal
3 large onions
5 cloves garlic
1 teaspoon curry if astrologically appropriate
½ pound bacon cut up (if astrologically appropriate, adds a nice flavor)
1 can tomato soup
1½ quarts water
⅓ cup sherry, or dark English-style ale
1 level tablespoon salt
3 tablespoons olive oil or 3 tablespoons butter or margarine
½ pound cut up mushrooms (if desired)

Chop the onions into fairly small pieces; cut the garlic very fine, squashing and mashing with the knife. Cut the veal into pieces about 1½ inches square. Put the oil or butter into a large pot and when sizzling hot put in the veal, bacon, onions and garlic and keep turning over and over until all is richly browned. (Don't have the heat too high and keep stirring to prevent burning). Then add the water, curry, tomato soup and sherry or ale. Slowly simmer for an hour, stirring occasionally to prevent it sticking. If fresh mushrooms are being used, add during the last 5 or 10 minutes of cooking. If using dried mushrooms, wash and add with the water. This dish can be prepared any time during the day. It reheats in 5 minutes and actually improves with reheating. Serves 8.

# WIENER SCHNITZEL

6 veal cutlets
1 teaspoon salt
¼ teaspoon pepper
1½ cups cracker crumbs
1 slightly beaten egg
1 tablespoon milk
½ cup hot water
2 tablespoons lemon juice
1 sliced hard boiled egg
6 lemon slices
   capers

Sprinkle veal with salt and pepper and pound well. Dip in crumbs, then in egg to which milk has been added, then in crumbs again and brown well in deep fat. Place in covered baking dish with hot water and cook in 400° F oven for 30 minutes. Sprinkle with lemon juice and serve garnished with hard boiled egg, lemon and capers. Serves 6.

# SCALOPPINE ALLA VALTELLINA

1½ pounds leg of veal
½ cup butter or margarine
   (¼ pound)
½ cup flour
½ cup Marsala wine
   (Marsala Florio is the
   best wine)
   salt and pepper
   astrologically appropriate herbs and spices
2 bay leaves
1 stalk celery
   Bel Paese cheese

The veal should be cut in thin slices about ½ inch thick and about 4 inches long, pounded with a mallet until ¼ inch thick. Dip the pieces of veal in the flour and press flour on both sides. Place the butter in a large frying pan and melt; then skim off the white curdled looking material that floats on the top. When the butter is clear and sizzling hot, put the veal in and quickly brown on both sides. When browned, lower heat and add the Marsala wine. When the scaloppine are cooked, pull a stalk of celery apart and first crushing the stalk with a knife put one piece, cut the length of the veal, on top of each piece of meat. Then place a thin slice of Bel Paese cheese on top of the celery. Put the scaloppine under the hot broiler until the cheese has melted and is slightly toasted. Serves 4.

# GHIVECI CU VIRGO

2½ to 3 pound veal cutlet
1 pound fresh tomatoes, or 1 can tomatoes
1 can tomato soup
1 clove garlic
1 pound fresh string beans; if fresh are not available, use frozen or 1 can string beans
2 tablespoons flour
1 medium onion
2 cups cold water butter or margarine salt and pepper

Melt butter in a baking pan. Salt and pepper veal cutlet and place it in the pan. Slice the tomatoes and place over the veal. Slice the garlic into small pieces and distribute through the tomatoes, then add ½ can of tomato soup and 1 cup of water. Bake at 375° F until cooked, about 1 hour.

Prepare string beans as follows: If fresh string beans are used, slice diagonally in thin slices and boil for 10 minutes. Drain. (Frozen string beans are cooked according to the package directions and drained.) Canned string beans do not have to be cooked and are simply drained. Fry the string beans with the sliced onion in butter for 10 minutes, then push to one side of the pan and in the cleared space add 2 tablespoons of flour, stirring constantly. Keep the frying pan half off the heat so that only the flour is browned, then add the other ½ can of tomato soup and cup of cold water. Mix all together, string beans, onions, tomato soup, water and browned flour. When boiling remove pan from heat and add to the meat and tomatoes in the baking dish, stirring gently and bake for another 20 minutes, when it will be ready to serve. Serves 4.

# LIBRA

## September 23 through October 22

*Ruling Element*
**Air**

*Ruling Planet*
**Venus**

*Nouriture*
**Cornucopia**

As a Libra, you constantly strive to maintain a harmonious balance within yourself and in your relationships with others. Unique among all the signs of the Zodiac, the nouriture of Libra is vegetarian. Many, indeed most, Libras do eat meat, but it is not part of the essence of their identity as Wild Game is for Leo, or Fish is for Pisces.

The nouriture of Libra is the Cornucopia itself. In ancient paintings and woodcuts from the Flemish plains to the hill towns of Italy, we see the balance scales of Libra rendered with fruits and vegetables, as well as grains, spilling across their platens.

With the Cornucopia as your nouriture, you are at home with every fruit, every vegetable and every grain that comes forth from the Earth, but there are certain specific ones above all, which are pivotal to the Libra identity. These include the fruits of Venus which you share with Taurus, specifically Apples, Avocados, Bananas, Blackberries, Cherries, Huckleberries, Peaches, Pears, Persimmons, Plums, Raspberries, Rhubarb and Strawberries, as well as Peas, Spinach and Tomatoes.

If you are a Libra of the First Decan, and you are intending to come into harmony with another person, using the fresh flavor of Wintergreen is extremely potent, as are the oils extracted from the peels of citrus fruits, particularly Lemons and Limes.

If you are a Libra of the Second Decan, you are the member of a very exclusive club. You are blessed as having been born during one of the four weeks of the year for which Tamarind and

Tarragon are the only spices. Take them. May they serve you well.

If you are a Libra of the Third Decan, and you are intending to come into harmony with another person, you may use virtually any herb that is grown on this Earth, but the most important are Bittersweet, Caraway, Clover, Dill, Fennel, Mint, Parsley, Peppermint, Anise, Cloves, Maple, Nutmeg, Sage and Sarsaparilla. Sassafras tea, especially when shared with someone else whose Decan prescribes this beverage, is sublime.

*Fruits*
Apples, Avocados, Bananas, Blackberries, Cherries, Huckleberries, Peaches, Pears, Persimmons, Plums, Raspberries, Rhubarb, Strawberries

*Vegetables*
Peas, Spinach, Tomatoes (listed as a vegetable, as it is used as such in contemporary cooking)

*Grains*
Barley, Corn, Oats, Rye, Wheat

*Herbs & Spices*

First Decan—September 23 through October 1: Wintergreen and the oils extracted from the peels of citrus fruits, particularly Lemons and Limes.

Second Decan—October 2 through 12: Tamarind, Tarragon

Third Decan—October 13 through 22: Bittersweet, Caraway, Clover, Dill, Fennel, Mint, Parsley, Peppermint, Anise, Cloves, Maple, Nutmeg, Sage, Sarsaparilla, Sassafras

# LIBRA'S HOME SOUP

1 cup dry split green peas
6 cups water
1 can bouillon
1 can tomato soup
  salt and pepper to taste

Place peas in a large saucepan without a lid and add 6 cups of cold water. Bring to the boiling point. Allow to simmer until the water cooks down and the peas are cooked to a soft, wet paste. Be careful not to let them burn. I find an aluminum pot best, as the peas are less likely to stick and burn.

Then add the 2 cans of soup, stir and allow to simmer for a few minutes. Season to taste, if necessary, after all the ingredients are added, as the canned soups are salted. If the soup is thicker than you prefer, just add a little water. Serves 4.

# STUFFED TOMATO SALAD

4 fresh medium tomatoes
1 stalk celery
1 apple
4 tablespoons
  mayonnaise
1 head lettuce

Peel the tomatoes, either by pouring boiling water over them or by holding them on a fork over an open flame for a few seconds. Cut out the stem mark and cut a good round opening. Then carefully scoop out most of the center of the tomatoes. Peel and carefully core the apple, and dice or cut into very little pieces. Cut into

small pieces an equal amount of celery. Sprinkle a little salt and paprika or pepper into the cavity in each tomato. Mix together the apple, celery, and mayonnaise. (If desired a little of the tomato removed from the center may be mixed in.) Fill each tomato with the mixture and serve on crisp lettuce leaves. Serves 4.

# EGGS BAKED IN TOMATOES

4　large tomatoes
4　eggs
　　salt and pepper
　　celery or onion salt
　　(optional)

Cut out the stem mark of large, ripe tomatoes and carefully scoop out most of pulp, enough to allow an egg to be poured in. Sprinkle inside the tomato with salt and pepper, adding celery or onion salt, if desired. Then break an egg into the tomato and put over it the chopped pulp. Place tomatoes in a pan and put this in another pan partially filled with water. On top of each tomato place a piece of brown paper heavily spread with butter. Bake at 375° F for 30 minutes. Serves 4.

# LIBRA SCRAMBLED EGGS

6　eggs
4　tablespoons cream
　　or milk
1　tablespoon tomato salsa
2　tablespoons chopped
　　tomato (optional)
1　tablespoon
　　Worcestershire sauce
½　teaspoon celery salt
½　teaspoon paprika
2　tablespoons butter or
　　margarine

Place in a bowl all the ingredients, except the butter, and beat with a rotary egg beater until thoroughly combined. Then melt the butter in a clean frying pan and when it starts to bubble pour in the egg mixture. As soon as the egg begins to cook on the bottom of the pan, gently scrape it off; use a tablespoon for this. As you scrape the cooked egg off the bottom of the pan, the liquid egg flows to bottom. Continue to slowly scrape it off the bottom of the pan until the whole mixture is of the exact consistency desired. Serve at once on hot plates. Do not let the scrambled egg stand in the frying pan or it will cook solid. Serves 4.

# SPAGHETTI LIBRA

2 pounds spaghetti or
  cappelini (angel hair)
5 fresh tomatoes
1 cup fresh peas
1 cup mushrooms
4 tablespoons olive oil (or
  butter or margarine)
1 large onion, chopped
  fine
2 teaspoons chili powder
  (if not available, use 2
  teaspoons Worcester-
  shire sauce and speck of
  cayenne pepper)
1 can beef bouillon or
  chicken consommé
  salt and pepper to taste

**Directions for sauce:**
Stew tomatoes and peas very slowly for thirty minutes. Meanwhile, cook slowly in a skillet the olive oil, or butter, and the onion for ten minutes. Drain the mushrooms and cut them into very small pieces, and add to the skillet. Add the tomatoes by pressing through a sieve with a spoon; add the chili powder, the bouillon, salt and pepper to taste. Then simmer very, very slowly for about one hour. Serve with hot spaghetti, noodles or macaroni, and serve with freshly grated Parmesan cheese.

**Directions for pasta:**
Put pasta in fast boiling salted water and boil for twenty minutes; then drain the water off and put a piece of butter in the pot (about one or two tablespoons, according to the amount of spaghetti, but not too much butter). When the water has drained out of the pasta, put it under the cold water faucet, and just let the cold water run over it for a moment, which washes out the excess starch, and immediately turn the spaghetti back into the pot in which you placed the butter. Then pour over the pasta the boiling hot sauce, and stir to thoroughly mix. Serve with freshly grated Parmesan cheese. Serves 4.

# SCALLOPED TOMATOES

3 cups cooked tomatoes
⅛ teaspoon pepper
½ teaspoon salt
2 teaspoons grated onion
2 cups bread crumbs
4 tablespoons butter or
   margarine
½ chopped green pepper

Add the green pepper, salt, pepper and onion to the tomatoes. Cover the bottom of a greased baking dish with bread crumbs. Add one half of the tomatoes and bits of butter. Cover with crumbs. Add the rest of the tomatoes, bits of butter and cover with crumbs. Dot with butter. Bake uncovered for 25 minutes at 375° F. Serves 4.

# TOMATO SAUCE

4 tablespoons butter or
   margarine
2 tablespoons finely
   chopped onion
2 tablespoons finely
   chopped celery
1 tablespoon finely
   chopped parsley
2 tablespoons flour
1 20-ounce can tomatoes
½ teaspoon salt
¼ teaspoon celery salt

Melt butter, then add the onion and celery and cook for 5 minutes; then add the flour and blend thoroughly; add the tomatoes, parsley, salt and celery salt, and allow the whole to slowly simmer for 30 minutes. Then pour and mash through wire sieve. Return to pot and heat to boiling point and serve. One teaspoon of A-1 or Worcestershire sauce can be added if desired.

# APPLE SAUCE AND STEWED APPLES

4 cups sliced apples
  (Granny Smiths or
  Pippins)
1 cup sugar (or less)
½ cup water

Put apples, sugar, and not more than ½ cup of water in saucepan. Cook over low heat until apples are tender. For sauce, mash the apples with a fork. A little nutmeg, lemon juice or clove will add to the flavor. Red cinnamon drops added while cooking will give a luscious cinnamon flavor and attractive pink color. Serves 4.

# BAYOU CREAMED GREEN PEAS

2½ cups shelled green peas
6 sprigs parsley
1 large bay leaf
1 large leaf or 2 small
  leaves fresh mint
1 whole clove
⅛ teaspoon pepper
2 tablespoons butter or
  margarine
½ cup scalded heavy
  cream
  minced parsley

Cook the green peas quickly in a little boiling salted water until tender, together with the parsley and bay leaf tied up with the other spices. Drain off the water, discard the bay leaf bouquet, and stir in 2 tablespoons of butter and ½ cup of scalded heavy cream. Bring to a boil and serve at once dusted with chopped parsley. Serves 4.

# SPLIT PEA PURÉE LIBRA

1 cup quick cooking
   split peas
2½ cups boiling water
   salt and white pepper
   dash nutmeg
2 tablespoons butter or
   margarine

Put the washed and picked split peas into the boiling water and boil gently for 25 minutes; rub through a sieve, season to taste with salt and white pepper and a dash of nutmeg, and stir in the butter. The purée should have the consistency of mashed potatoes. It may be kept for several days in the refrigerator if desired. Serves 4.

# SPLIT PEA VEGETARIAN SAUSAGE

1 cup Split Pea Purée
   Libra (recipe above)
½ cup dried fine bread
   crumbs
2 tablespoons heavy
   sweet cream or Cream
   Sauce (recipe on
   page 79)
   salt and pepper to taste
½ teaspoon powdered
   sage

1 egg
2 teaspoons
   Worcestershire sauce
1 tablespoon grated
   onion
½ small clove garlic,
   mashed to a pulp
2 tablespoons butter or
   margarine

Mix the ingredients together. Shape in form of small sausages; roll in fine bread crumbs and fry in butter until brown. Serve with fried apple or pineapple rings and cucumber relish. Serves 4.

# SCORPIO

## October 23 through November 21

| Ruling Element | Ruling Planet | Nouriture |
|---|---|---|
| **Water** | **Mars** | **Shellfish** |

As a Scorpio, you are assertive, fearless and filled with confidence, all characteristics which befit a person whose sign is ruled by Mars. You have an expansive nature, and your nouriture is one of the broadest of all the signs of the Zodiac.

As with the other Water signs, Cancer and Pisces, your nouriture is *of* the water. All the fruits of the sea are divided among the three water signs, the Fish to Pisces, the Crab to Cancer, and all other Shellfish to Scorpio. The nouriture of Scorpio includes (but is not limited to) Calamari, Clams, Lobsters, Oysters, Scallops and all the soups, stews and chowders made from them.

At the same time, Scorpio's nouriture includes Carrots, Hops, Onions, Peppers, Pimentos, Radishes and Shallots as well as Pumpkins. There is probably no one fruit or vegetable that is more closely associated with a single holiday than the pumpkin is associated with All Hallow's Eve (Hallowe'en). With this in mind, it is certainly appropriate that the pumpkin be associated with the sign of the Zodiac within whose influence October 31 is found.

Scorpio's broad nouriture also includes the bitterest as well as the largest fruits: Grapefruit and Watermelon.

If you are a Scorpio of the First Decan, and you are intending to come into harmony with another person, you have a choice of Allspice, Basil, Chili Pepper, Coriander, Cumin, Curry, Garlic, Ginger, Horseradish, Mustard, Pepper, Peppermint, Cardamom, Licorice, Sage, Spearmint, Sugar, Thyme and Vanilla.

If you are a Scorpio of the Second Decan, and you are intending to come into harmony with another person, you have a choice of spices which is nearly as broad as your preceding sister Decan. You may use Bay leaves, Chamomile, Chicory, Cinnamon, Citron, Ginseng, Rosemary, Saffron, Sesame, Anise, Cloves, Maple, Nutmeg, Sage and Sarsaparilla. Both Chamomile and Sassafras teas are also very effective.

Pumpkin pies baked before midnight on Hallowe'en should be flavored with Vanilla, while pies that come out of the oven after midnight may appropriately be made with Nutmeg and Cinnamon.

The Licorice flavor that is popular at this time may be achieved with Licorice root before midnight, and with Anise after midnight. In the Third Decan of Scorpio, one returns to Licorice root.

If you are a Scorpio of the Third Decan, and you are intending to come into harmony with another person, you may use, in addition to pure Licorice, Cardamom, Sage, Spearmint, Thyme, Vanilla, Wintergreen and the oils extracted from the peels of Lemons.

# SCORPIO

*Fruits*
Grapefruit, Watermelon

*Vegetables*
Carrots, Hops, Onions, Peppers, Pimentos, Pumpkins, Radishes, Shallots

*Herbs & Spices*

First Decan—October 23 through 31:
Allspice, Basil, Chili Pepper, Coriander, Cumin, Curry, Garlic, Ginger, Horseradish, Mustard, Pepper, Peppermint, Cardamom, Licorice, Sage, Spearmint, Thyme, Vanilla

Second Decan—November 1 through 10:
Bay leaves, Chamomile, Chicory, Cinnamon, Citron, Ginseng, Rosemary, Saffron, Sesame, Anise, Cloves, Maple, Nutmeg, Sage, Sarsaparilla, Sassafras

Third Decan—November 11 through 21:
Cardamom, Licorice, Sage, Spearmint, Thyme, Vanilla, Wintergreen, Lemon peel

# QUICK ONION SOUP

1 large Spanish onion
2 cans consommé
1 can bouillon
  French bread sliced and
  toasted, or rusks
  grated Parmesan
  cheese
2 tablespoons butter or
  margarine

Cut the Spanish onion into slices, a little less than ¼ inch thick, and cross cut the slices. Put the butter in a frying pan or pot and when sizzling hot put the sliced onion in. Lower flame and let onion slowly cook for 10 minutes, turning the onion over once or twice. The onion should not be browned, but cooked soft; then add to canned soups and allow to cook for 5 minutes. Season to taste, but do not add any seasoning without first tasting, as some canned consommé and other soups are quite highly seasoned.

If served from a tureen at the table, place in the tureen the toasted slices of French bread or the rusks, and pour the soup over them. If served directly into plates, place the pieces of toast into hot plates and pour in the soup. Serve with grated Parmesan cheese, or other good grated cheese. Serves 4.

# LOBSTER BISQUE

2 tablespoons butter or
  margarine
1 pound lobster or 1 can
  lobster
3 cups cream or milk
  salt and pepper

Heat butter in a pan. Do not brown. Add the lobster. Cook 3 minutes. Stir into this the cream or milk. Dust with salt and pepper. Serve very hot with finger rolls that have been split, buttered and toasted. Serves 4.

# PASTA WITH CLAM SAUCE

½ cup butter or
  margarine (¼ pound)
½ cup Italian olive oil
2 finely chopped
  medium onions
1 20-ounce can Italian
  tomatoes
1 tablespoon Italian
  tomato paste
3 or 4 bay leaves
6 large clams
1 clove garlic, chopped
  fine and crushed with
  a knife
  speck of cayenne
  salt and pepper

**Directions for sauce:**

Fry onions and garlic in butter and oil, until of golden color. While onions are cooking, put contents of tomato can in a little bowl and break up the tomatoes; when onions are a golden color, add the tomatoes. Dissolve tomato paste in ¾ cup of hot water and add to sauce. Put some of the water or juices of the clams into this mixture. Add bay leaves and seasoning. Let this cook very slowly for at least half an hour. (The longer it cooks the better.) Chop up the clams into very small pieces, conserving all juices, and 5 minutes before serving add clams to sauce.

The above recipe can be made with 8 mussels, instead of clams; this is typically Italian.

**Directions for pasta:**

Put pasta in fast boiling salted water and boil for twenty minutes; then drain the water off and put a piece of butter in the pot (about one or two tablespoons, according to the amount of spaghetti, but not too much butter). When the water has drained out of the pasta, put it under the cold water faucet, and just let the cold water run over it for a moment, which washes out the excess starch, and immediately turn the spaghetti back into the pot in which you placed the butter. Then pour over the pasta the boiling hot sauce, and stir to thoroughly mix. Serve with freshly grated Parmesan cheese. Serves 4.

# STUFFED RED PEPPERS

| | |
|---|---|
| 7 | sweet red peppers |
| 2 | cups water |
| 1 | cup vinegar |
| ½ | cup sugar |
| 4 | whole cloves |
| 2 | finely chopped unpeeled apples |
| 2 | cups finely chopped cabbage |
| 1 | cup cream |
| ½ | teaspoon salt |
| 4 | teaspoons sugar |
| 2 | tablespoons orange juice |
| 4 | tablespoons lemon juice |

Remove the seeds from peppers, leaving them whole. Boil 5 minutes in water, vinegar, ½ cup sugar and 4 cloves. Drain and chill. Stuff 6 peppers with the following mixture: Chopped apples, cabbage and one pepper chopped fine.

Dress this with the following: Cream, salt, 4 teaspoons sugar, orange juice and lemon juice. Beat thoroughly until stiff. Mix with the chopped ingredients. Stuff the peppers. Serve with toasted cheese crackers. Serves 6.

# SHRIMP SAUCE

| | |
|---|---|
| ½ | cup butter or margarine (¼ pound) |
| 4 | level tablespoons flour |
| 1½ | cups hot water |
| 1 | teaspoon salt |
| ⅛ | teaspoon pepper |
| 2 | egg yolks |
| ½ | cup canned or boiled shrimp |

Melt butter and add flour. Stir to thoroughly blend. Then add hot water, place over low heat, add seasonings and stir till the mixture boils (or if cooked in double boiler, stir till the mixture thickens). Allow to cook slowly for 30 minutes, stirring every now and then. When cooked 30 minutes pour over slightly beaten yolks of eggs. Add shrimp broken in pieces and serve with fish as desired.

# BAKED SHRIMP

2 cups shrimp
2 tablespoons butter or
  margarine
2 tablespoons flour
½ cup cooking wine or
  orange juice
1½ cups milk

  lemon peel
½ teaspoon salt
  pepper
  mace
2 well beaten eggs
  cracker crumbs

Wash and drain the shrimp. Heat the butter in a pan and heat the shrimp in this. Stir in the flour. Add the milk. Stir well and cook until bubbling. Add the wine or orange juice, a bit of lemon peel, salt, pepper to taste and a sprinkling of mace. Stir in the well beaten eggs. Place in an open casserole and cover the top with buttered cracker crumbs. Bake 20 minutes at 375° F. Serves 4.

# HORSERADISH SAUCE

1 tablespoon butter or
  margarine
1 tablespoon flour
1 cup milk
¼ cup freshly grated
  horseradish
¼ cup soft bread crumbs
  (no crust)
½ teaspoon salt
½ teaspoon paprika
2 tablespoons lemon juice
1 tablespoon vinegar

Make white cream sauce by melting the butter and adding the flour. Stir to thoroughly blend (with no lumps). Add the milk and bring to the boiling point, stirring constantly. Allow to slowly simmer for 3 minutes to remove the raw starch taste. Then add the horseradish, bread crumbs, salt and paprika and allow to simmer for 2 minutes, stirring constantly. Then remove from heat and add lemon juice and vinegar. Serve with the appropriate meats and shellfish.

# SHRIMP ALLA SCORPIO

1½ pounds fresh shrimp (if fresh not available, use the equivalent in canned shrimp)
½ cup butter or margarine (¼ pound)
½ cup green olive oil
2 finely chopped large onions
3 finely chopped leeks
1 finely chopped small clove garlic
¼ cup finely chopped chives
1 small can tomatoes
2 level tablespoons tomato paste
2 cubes bouillon
½ cup boiling water
2 cups white wine
2 tablespoons finely chopped parsley and/or astrologically appropriate herbs and spices
4 tablespoons butter
¼ teaspoon cayenne pepper
salt and pepper to taste

Put the ½ cup of butter and olive oil into a large pot. When hot, put in the finely chopped onions, garlic, leeks and chives. When they begin to get golden, put in the shrimp. When they get pink, add the wine, salt, pepper and cayenne and cook for 10 minutes over moderate heat. Take out the shrimp and add the tomatoes and tomato paste. Cook for 5 minutes, still over moderate heat, then strain all the material through a wire sieve into another pot, pressing everything through the sieve with a large spoon, using a great deal of force until all is forced through. Then add the bouillon dissolved in water, and allow the whole mixture to boil until it is reduced by about one third. It should then be a fairly thick sauce. While the sauce is reducing, remove the shells from the shrimp. Just before serving, return the shrimp and add the parsley to the sauce. Last, add 4 tablespoons butter. When it melts, serve. Serves 4.

# HOMARD SCORPIO

8 pounds lobster
1½ cups butter or
  margarine (¾ pound)
  (½ cup of this is used
  just before serving)
1 cup fine olive oil
  (green olive oil)
6 leeks
4 large onions
½ bundle of chives
3 large fresh tomatoes or
  ½ can tomatoes
3 bouillon cubes
½ cup brandy
4 cups dry white wine
  (1 quart)
3 tablespoons finely
  chopped parsley
  cayenne pepper
  (important, as dish
  should be slightly hot)
  salt and pepper

Chop up very finely the onions, leeks (using the white and a small part of the green of the leeks) and chives. Put into a large pot 1 cup of butter (½ pound) and the olive oil. When sizzling hot, put in the chopped onion mixture and fry until the onions begin to turn a golden color. Then add the lobster pieces, salt, pepper and a pinch of cayenne. Cook until the lobster shell turns red. Then pour in ½ cup of brandy. Simmer gently and add the tomatoes. Cook for five minutes. Add the white wine and cook for a further ten minutes over moderate heat. Then take the lobsters out and keep in a warm place while you make a sauce from the liquid in the pot. This is done, as follows: Pour all the remaining materials from the pot into a wire sieve, which should be placed over another pot. Reserve liquid. Then force all the materials through the sieve, mashing completely. (Or you may purée in the blender.) Now add to this sauce three cubes of bouillon, which have been dissolved in a cup of boiling water and boil the whole mixture until the quantity is reduced by about one third. Then, just before serving, add 2 cups of the reserved juices from the lobster and let come to a boil. Add ¼ cup of butter and the finely chopped parsley and pour all the sauce over the lobsters and serve. Serves 6.

# SAGITTARIUS

## November 22 through December 21

| *Ruling Element* | *Ruling Planet* | *Nouriture* |
|:---:|:---:|:---:|
| **Fire** | **Jupiter** | **Ham, Pork, Sausages** |

As a Sagittarius, you are active, a seeker and a hunter. As with Leo, a fellow fire sign, you have a rich, though not extensive, nouriture. Unless you have chosen to lead a vegetarian life, your nouriture includes Ham, Pork, and especially Sausages of all types. Again, as with Leo, the full richness is experienced when your main dish is cooked over an open fire.

Specific spices are appropriate for each of the Sagittarian Decans. In the First Decan it is Dill or Fennel. In the Second Decan it is Basil or Garlic, and in the Third Decan it is Rosemary or Tarragon.

As with Pisces, with whom you share these fruits of the Earth, your vegetables are Artichokes, Brussels Sprouts, Endives and Kale and your fruits are Dates, Figs and Mangos.

The figs may appear in desserts or complementing your main dish on the table's primary platter. Chestnuts may also be part of this presentation.

If you are a Sagittarian of the First Decan, and you are intending to come into harmony with another person, you may choose from Bittersweet, Caraway, Clover, Dill, Fennel, Mint, Parsley or Peppermint to flavor the dishes of her or his primary sign.

If you are a Sagittarian of the Second Decan, and you are intending to come into harmony with another person, you may choose from Allspice, Basil, Chili Pepper, Coriander, Cumin, Curry, Garlic, Ginger, Horseradish, Mustard, Pepper, Peppermint, Wintergreen, or Lemon peel to flavor the dishes of her or his primary sign.

## SAGITTARIUS

*Fruits*
Dates, Figs, Mangos

*Vegetables*
Artichokes, Brussels Sprouts, Endives, Kale

*Nuts*
Chestnuts

*Herbs & Spices*

First Decan—November 22 through December 2: Bittersweet, Caraway, Clover, Dill, Fennel, Mint, Parsley, Peppermint

Second Decan—December 3 through 11: Allspice, Basil, Chili Pepper, Coriander, Cumin, Curry, Garlic, Ginger, Horseradish, Mustard, Pepper, Peppermint, Wintergreen, Lemon peel

Third Decan—December 12 through 21: Bay leaves, Chamomile, Chicory, Cinnamon, Citron, Ginseng, Rosemary, Saffron, Sesame

If you are a Sagittarian of the Third Decan, and you are intending to come into harmony with another person, use Bay leaves, Chamomile, Chicory, Citron, Ginseng, Rosemary, Saffron or Sesame to flavor the main dishes that you prepare for them, and use Cinnamon to add that special flavor to dessert.

# LUNCHEON SOUP

2 tablespoons butter or
  margarine
½ cup minced ham
1 sliced onion
½ teaspoon curry powder
2 tablespoons minced
  unpeeled apple
2 cups water

2 tablespoons minced
  celery
  juice of ½ lemon
1 teaspoon grated
  lemon peel
1 cup boiled and
  minced potato
½ teaspoon salt
2 cups milk

Heat the butter in a saucepan at gentle heat. Add the onion, apple and celery. Cook covered for 5 minutes. Add the boiled potato, ham, curry powder and water. Simmer 5 minutes. Add the lemon juice, lemon peel, salt and milk. Simmer 5 minutes. Serve with squares of toast and grated cheese or crackers and cheese. Decorate with minced parsley and a slice of lemon that has been dusted with paprika. Serves 4.

# WATERCRESS AND FIG SALAD

1 bundle watercress
1 mango
1 cup figs
2 ounces chopped
  chestnuts (¼ pound
  nuts will serve about 8)

Cut the mango in halves, remove seed and chop fine. Divide figs in half, then cut in slices. Wash watercress, removing long stems.

Now place the salad together as follows: Divide the watercress on four plates (or it can be divided on six). Over each plate of watercress place a few thin slices of fig; then scatter over each plate a quarter of the chopped mango and over all sprinkle chopped chestnuts. Serves 4.

# BRUSSELS SPROUTS WITH CHESTNUTS

4   cups Brussels sprouts
½   pound large chestnuts
¼   cup butter or margarine
     salt and black pepper
     to taste
     ground nutmeg
¾   cup Cream Sauce
     (recipe on page 79)

Boil the Brussels sprouts in salted water for 10 minutes. Meanwhile cover the chestnuts with boiling water and boil for 15 minutes, or until soft; drain. Peel off both the outer shell and the thin brown inside skin. Cut the chestnuts into quarters. Drain the cooked sprouts well; add the chestnuts, butter, salt, black pepper, dash of nutmeg and Cream Sauce (recipe on page 79). Let stand in a double boiler or over a very low heat for 5 minutes, then serve very hot. Serves 6.

# PORK TENDERLOIN

1   boneless pork
     tenderloin (allow ⅓
     pound per serving)
     flour
     salt and pepper to taste
2   tablespoons butter or
     margarine
     astrologically appropri-
     ate herbs and spices
     juice of 1 lemon
1   cup milk
1   slice onion
     sliced mushrooms
     (optional)
     minced parsley

The pork should be cut into rounds. Dust with flour, salt, pepper, herbs and spices. Brown in hot butter. Add the lemon juice, milk and onion. Cook covered, slowly, for 20 minutes. Mushrooms may be added 10 minutes before serving. Sprinkle with minced parsley when ready to serve.

# RAVIOLI SAGITTARIUS

## FILLING

4 quarts spinach (16 cups)
2 pounds fresh sausage
8 eggs
3 cups grated Parmesan
  cheese

1 cup finely grated bread
  crumbs, or cracker
  crumbs
1 cup finely chopped
  chestnuts
3 tablespoons olive oil
  salt and pepper to taste
1 teaspoon marjoram

Wash the spinach thoroughly. Place in a large pot of water, bring to a boil and cook for 10 minutes. Drain and cool. Squeeze dry and chop very fine. Beat the eggs gently and add to the spinach. Then add the cheese, bread crumbs, olive oil and marjoram. Add salt and pepper to taste. Mix well and refrigerate for 24 hours.

## DOUGH

2 cups sifted flour
3 eggs
3 tablespoons water
1 tablespoon salt

Sift flour and salt into a large bowl. Make hollow in center of flour and break into this the eggs and water. With a knife or pastry knife mix these ingredients together, cutting through the eggs and mixing until combined in a heavy, rather dry dough. It may be necessary to add just a trifle more water, being careful to add only just enough to make the flour and egg mixture combine. Next sprinkle some flour over your pastry board, or table top (be sure it's a good level surface). Rub flour over your hands. Then lift the dough from the bowl and place it on the floured dough board, or table, and knead the dough. This is done by pressing the knuckles through the dough and pulling the dough over into one lump and pressing the knuckles through it again. Knead the dough with both hands until the dough does not stick to either the table or your hands. Then divide it into 4 pieces. Roll out the first piece of dough, rolling in all directions from the center out—roll away from you all the time and turn the dough around as you roll. Continue to roll until the dough is the thickness of heavy paper. Each sheet of dough should be filled with the filling before rolling the next sheet out.

## Combining Dough and Filling:

Onto the sheet of dough place a row of rounded tablespoons of the filling, about 1 inch apart, and far enough from the top of the sheet to allow for the top of the dough to be turned over and cover them. Cut the dough immediately below the filling, leaving enough edge to join with the piece that was turned over. With the side of your hand press the dough together and across between each filling. Then cut across, separating each piece of dough with filling and carefully press together the edges on each of the 3 cut sides. You now have separate little filled pockets of dough, which can be made either in squares or diamond shapes. Continue to do this until all the filling is used.

## Cooking Directions:

Place the ravioli into rapidly boiling salted water, a few at a time, to avoid stopping the boiling. Allow to boil for about 20 minutes (according to the size of the ravioli). Serve with grated Parmesan cheese and butter or margarine. Serves 8.

# BAKED HAM CASSEROLE

1 large slice ham
6 sliced figs
3 large sweet potatoes
4 mangos
1 cup mango nectar
   or juice
   brown sugar
   butter or margarine

Cover the bottom of a casserole with sliced figs. Peel and cut the sweet potatoes into lengthwise slices, layering over the figs. Peel and slice the mangos, removing the pits. Layer over the sweet potatoes. Put the ham over all. Add the mango nectar or juice and cook covered for 2 hours in a 300° F oven. Uncover and sprinkle generously with brown sugar and butter. Brown under the broiler. Serves 4.

# BAKED SLICED HAM AND MANGOS

2 large, thin slices raw or
   smoked ham (¼ to ⅓
   inch thick)
1 teaspoon dry mustard
2 teaspoons vinegar
1 mango
½ cup brown sugar
   butter or margarine

Mix together the mustard and vinegar. Spread the mixture thinly on the ham. Peel, remove pit and slice mango very thin, spreading 2 layers of the thin slices on ham. Sprinkle well with brown sugar. Now roll the ham the long way, starting from the fat side and rolling the fat into the center. Hold together with metal butcher skewers. Place in baking pan and put a few dabs of butter on each ham roll. Bake at 375° F for 25 minutes. Baste 2 or 3 times while baking. Serves 4.

# SCALLOPED HAM & EGGS

1 slice raw or smoked
  ham
½ small onion
  butter or margarine
2 hard boiled eggs
1 cup Cream Sauce
  (canned or recipe
  below)
½ tablespoon
  Worcestershire sauce
1 tablespoon grated
  Parmesan cheese

Place ham in small baking dish. Sprinkle the finely chopped onion on it and place a few dabs of butter on top. Bake at 425° F for 15 minutes. Cut hard boiled eggs in slices. Remove ham from oven and put slices of egg all over it. Add the Worcestershire to Cream Sauce (see below) and pour over all. Sprinkle the grated Parmesan cheese over the sauce and return to oven to melt the cheese. Serves 8.

# CREAM SAUCE

2 tablespoons butter or
  margarine or shortening
2 tablespoons flour
1 cup milk
¼ teaspoon salt or season
  to taste
⅛ teaspoon pepper or
  season to taste

Melt butter or shortening in upper part of double boiler, or over low heat. Add flour and stir until well blended. Pour the milk in, stirring constantly until the sauce thickens. Add salt and pepper and stir thoroughly. Cook until the raw starch taste has left the sauce, 3 to 5 minutes.

# CAPRICORN

## December 22 through January 20

| *Ruling Element* | *Ruling Planet* | *Nouriture* |
|:---:|:---:|:---:|
| **Earth** | **Saturn** | **Lamb** |

As a Capricorn, you are a deep thinker, deliberate in thought and action. As such, you should be able to do a masterful job in preparing any of the appropriate meals in this book. Your own dishes, which you have in common with your neighboring Aquarians, offer the opportunity for broad complexity. Indeed, vegetables such as Beets, Eggplant or Zucchini may be prepared in a variety of creative ways.

Your fruits, such as Cantaloupe and Honeydew melons, may be eaten as picked or used as the centerpieces of elaborate fruit salads. Quinces, meanwhile, are one of the more exotic fruits associated with any sign of the Zodiac.

If you are a Capricorn of the First Decan, and you are intending to come into harmony with another person, use Anise, Cloves, Maple, Nutmeg, Sage or Sarsaparilla to flavor the dishes of her or his primary sign. Sassafras tea is also effective in achieving harmony with persons whose own Decan prescribes Sassafras.

If you are a Capricorn of the Second Decan, and you are intending to come into harmony with another person, don't hold back. Choose from Allspice, Basil, Chili Pepper, Coriander, Cumin, Curry, Garlic, Ginger, Horseradish, Mustard, Pepper, Sage, or Thyme to flavor the main dishes that you prepare for her or him. Cardamom, used in the cuisine of India, is also one of your spices. For dessert, or for other special times, choose from Licorice, Peppermint, Spearmint or Vanilla.

If you are a Capricorn of the Third Decan, and you are intending to come into harmony with another person, you should focus on such

## CAPRICORN

*Fruits*
Cantaloupe, Honeydew melons,
Quinces

*Vegetables*
Beets, Eggplant, Zucchini

*Herbs & Spices*

First Decan—December 22 through
December 31: Anise, Cloves, Maple,
Nutmeg, Sage, Sarsaparilla, Sassafras

Second Decan—January 1 through 11:
Allspice, Basil, Chili Pepper, Coriander,
Cumin, Curry, Garlic, Ginger, Horse-
radish, Mustard, Pepper, Peppermint,
Cardamom, Licorice, Sage, Spearmint,
Thyme, Vanilla

Third Decan—January 12 through 20:
Bittersweet, Caraway, Clover, Dill, Fen-
nel, Mint, Parsley, Peppermint, Bay,
Chamomile, Chicory, Cinnamon, Citron,
Ginseng, Rosemary, Saffron, Sesame

flavorings as Bittersweet, Caraway, Clover,
Dill, Fennel, Mint, Parsley, Peppermint, Bay,
Chicory, Cinnamon, Citron, Rosemary, Saffron
or Sesame. You may be surprised with the re-
sults of sharing a nice pot of Chamomile or
Ginseng tea.

# BEET SOUP

| | |
|---|---|
| 1 | can beets |
| ½ | cup water |
| 1 | cup chicken bouillon |
| 2 | cups milk |
| ¼ | teaspoon salt |
| | celery salt |
| | whipped cream |
| | finely minced parsley |

Mince beets fine, reserving juice. Add water to the juice. Simmer the beets and liquid 10 minutes. Strain. Add the chicken bouillon, milk and salt. Dust with celery salt. Add whipped cream to the top of each serving. Sprinkle with minced parsley. Serves 4.

# STUFFED EGGPLANT

| | |
|---|---|
| 1 | eggplant |
| ¼ | cup chopped onion |
| 1 | cup cooked |
| | chopped lamb |
| 1 | cup mushrooms |
| ¼ | teaspoon salt |
| ⅛ | teaspoon pepper |
| 4 | tablespoons butter or |
| | margarine |
| | buttered bread crumbs |

Cut the top from the eggplant. Scoop out the pulp leaving a shell ½ inch thick. Wash the mushrooms. Chop them with the eggplant. Add the onions. Sauté the vegetables in the butter for 10 minutes. Add the chopped lamb and seasoning.

Fill the eggplant. Cover the top with buttered crumbs. Bake in a buttered dish, uncovered, at 400° F for the first 10 minutes. Then reduce the heat to 375° F and bake for 25 minutes. Serves 4.

# BEETS IN ORANGE SAUCE

3 tablespoons grated
  orange rind
2 tablespoons lemon juice
⅓ teaspoon salt
  black pepper
  nutmeg
1 tablespoon flour
1 tablespoon sherry
⅓ cup butter or margarine
3½ cups cooked and
  sliced beets
  finely chopped parsley
  astrologically appropriate herbs and spices

Combine the grated orange rind, lemon juice, salt, and a dash each of black pepper and nutmeg. Stir in 1 scant tablespoon of flour. Blend until smooth, adding the sherry. Cook in top of a double boiler, over hot water, stirring frequently until thickened. Let simmer gently for 10 minutes, stirring occasionally, and when ready to use, add the butter and stir until melted. Finally add the cooked, sliced beets; heat through, and serve in a hot vegetable dish dusting with finely chopped parsley or other appropriate herbs and spices. Serves 4.

# KALE

1 head of kale
2 cups boiling water
1 teaspoon salt
  butter or margarine
  salt and pepper
  sliced hard boiled eggs
  (optional)

Remove the root and the heavy part of the leaf. Wash and soak in warm water. Lift carefully from the water. Cook, closely covered, in the boiling water with 1 teaspoon salt. Cook 35 to 40 minutes. Drain. Chop. Season with salt, pepper and butter. Decorate with sliced hard-boiled eggs. Serves 4.

# DOLMA CAPRICORN

2 small or 1 large
   eggplant
1 pound stewing lamb
1 medium onion
¾ cup rice
½ cup seedless raisins
¼ cup pine nuts
2 tablespoons butter or
   margarine
¼ cup flour
  salt
  pepper

Cut lamb in pieces, sprinkle with salt, sift flour over each piece and press it in. Place the butter (or other fat, if you prefer) in frying pan and when sizzling hot add the lamb and brown on each side. Then add enough water to completely cover the lamb, adding the onion, salt and pepper to taste and slowly simmer 30 minutes, while you boil the rice and prepare the eggplant. Boil about 2 quarts of water in a large pot with 2 level tablespoons of salt. Wash rice thoroughly in cold water, then drain and sprinkle into the rapidly boiling salted water. Cook uncovered until the rice is tender. In the meantime, prepare the eggplant. Remove the stem and cut off a small part of the eggplant and with a teaspoon dig out the inside, leaving a shell about 1 inch or 1¼ inches thick.

To prepare the stuffing, cut up some of the cooked lamb into little pieces, until you have a cupful; it is better not to use the fat, or very little of it. Pour the remainder of the meat and gravy into a large pot that has a lid. The pot should be just large enough to enable you to boil the eggplant in the stew gravy when it is stuffed. Allow the balance of the stew or liquid to continue slowly simmering. Next, strain the water from the rice (it should be tender) and run plenty of cold water over it to remove the excess starch. Then put into a bowl the rice, cooked lamb, raisins and pine nuts. Mix these ingredients together and salt and pepper to taste. It is important that you season well, as some of the seasoning will go into the eggplant, which is not seasoned otherwise.

Pack the stuffing into the eggplant as tightly as possible. Place the stuffed eggplant into the pot with the boiling stew;

there should be enough liquid to float the eggplant (it won't sink all the way into the liquid, but float). If necessary, add boiling water and season to taste. Cover the pot and allow to very slowly boil until the eggplant is very soft when tested with a fork. Serve without any other vegetable. Carve across the eggplant, cutting and serving it in thick slices. This is a very delicious and unusual dish and is quite easy to prepare.

The liquid that is left can be served the following day as a soup. If there is any meat left, cut it into small pieces. If any stuffing material is left over, add it; if not, add a little rice and allow it to cook until quite soft and tender. The extra eggplant that was dug out can be fried or baked in a little butter and added to the soup. A little tomato can be added, if desired. Chill the liquid and remove the fat from the top. Reheat and serve. Serves 4.

# SCHASCHLYK CAPRICORN

1½  pounds lamb steak
1  cup vinegar
1⅓  cups water
3  bay leaves
1½  teaspoons salt
1½  teaspoons sugar
2  medium yellow or
    red onions
1  very small clove garlic,
    or few thin slices
6  tomatoes or 18 cherry
    tomatoes
1  bunch scallions
    (spring onions)
1  lemon

Pour into a saucepan the vinegar and water (there should be just a little more water than vinegar); add 3 bay leaves and the salt and sugar. Bring the mixture to the boiling point and allow to very slowly boil for about 5 minutes; then cool. Next cut the meat into small squares, not more than 1 inch square. Slice the onions and cut the garlic into halves. If you do not have a small clove, then use 2 or 3 thin slices cut from a larger clove. Now place the meat, the onion and the garlic into the cold vinegar and water. (I am aware of the fact that some just cover the meat with uncooked vinegar and water, but this is not correct and will not give the desired result); there should be enough of the vinegar and water to just cover the meat. Place in refrigerator and allow to soak in this mixture for 24 hours, or until ready to cook.

Remove meat from liquid and allow to drain. Cut tomatoes into thick slices and sprinkle a little salt and pepper on

(continued on page 86)

them, but not on the meat, because it has been seasoned in the vinegar mixture. Use the cherry tomatoes whole. Using the regular 5- or 6-inch long wire meat skewers put on a piece of meat, a slice of tomato, another piece of meat and so on, alternating with meat and slices of tomato until the skewers are filled. In placing the meat on the skewers, place all fat on the pieces of meat on the same side, because when you broil these under the flame or over a heat the fat should be on top, so that as it melts, it trickles down over the broiling meat, keeping it moist and flavoring it. Broil over a hot heat or under a fast flame for about 15 to 20 minutes, according to how well done you like the meat. Broil on one side and then turn when first side is browned. Push the meat and tomatoes off the skewers onto the plates and put a quarter lemon on each plate. The lemon should be squeezed over the meat before eating. Serve with this dish one bunch of scallions (spring onions) that have been cut up fine; cut up the white and a part of the green. Serve no other vegetable. Serves 4.

# LAMB KALDOLMAR KAPRICORN

| | |
|---|---|
| 1 | medium head cabbage |
| 1 | pound lean ground lamb |
| 1 | medium onion |
| 3 | medium tomatoes or 1 small can tomatoes |
| 2 | tablespoons rice |
| 1 | egg |
| 3 or 4 | bay leaves |
| 2 | tablespoons sage |
| 1 | cup sweet cream |
| 2 to 4 | tablespoons sifted flour |
| 3 or 4 | tablespoons butter or margarine or bacon fat boiling water |

Boil cabbage whole, first cutting the stem out. This is done because you have to take the leaves off and use them whole. Let cabbage boil uncovered for 15 minutes in rapidly boiling water. As soon as cabbage is put on to cook, wash the rice and sprinkle into another pot of boiling water and cook 15 minutes. Cut the onion into very small pieces and sauté it lightly in butter.

Remove both the rice and cabbage from heat and strain. Then mix ingredients as follows: Put in a bowl the lamb, rice, onion, egg, salt and pepper and mix into a kind of paste, then roll into oblong rolls, using about a rounded tablespoon in each roll.

Next separate the leaves of the cabbage and roll each meat roll in a cabbage leaf, fastening with toothpicks. If you are making a large quantity put less meat into each cabbage leaf as the leaves get smaller.

Now put 3 tablespoons of butter or bacon fat (personally I use butter) into a large pot on the stove and fry the rolls of cabbage and meat on top and bottom until browned. Then add enough boiling water to cover the cabbage and meat rolls. Add salt and pepper to taste, bay leaves, sage and diced tomatoes. Cover and allow to simmer for at least 1 hour. Then add 2 level tablespoons of flour to the sweet cream and beat slightly with rotary egg beater or purée in the blender to avoid lumpy gravy. Remove the cabbage and meat rolls from the gravy and put them on a hot platter. Then add the cream and flour to the gravy and stir it in. Let it boil about 5 minutes, stirring constantly, then pour over the cabbage and meat balls. Serve with boiled potatoes and delicious hot biscuits. Serves 4.

# LAMB POT ROAST

| | |
|---|---|
| 4 | pounds lamb shoulder |
| 2 | tablespoons butter or margarine |
| 2 | sliced tomatoes |
| 1 | cup celery |
| 4 | minced carrots |
| 2 | sliced onions |
| 1 | thin slice garlic |
| 2 or 3 | cups water |
| 2 | tablespoons flour |

Have the butcher bone the lamb and remove every trace of fat. Have the meat rolled and bound in a compact mass. Brown it in butter until a rich, deep brown. Place in a kettle. Surround this with the vegetables. Add the water to the pan the meat was browned in. Pour over the vegetables. Add more hot water if necessary. The water should half cover the pot roast. Cook slowly for 2 hours. Remove the meat. Make a sauce of the vegetables and liquid in the pan by adding the flour mixed with 4 tablespoons of water. Serve with Broiled Eggplant (recipe on page 93). Serves 8.

# AQUARIUS

## January 21 through February 19

| Ruling Element | Ruling Planet | Nouriture |
|:---:|:---:|:---:|
| **Air** | **Saturn** | **Seafood** |

As an Aquarius, you are reserved and compassionate, yet powerful. As the Water Bearer, you draw your nouriture *from* the water, and as such, you bear a special relationship to the three water signs, whose nouriture is *of* the water. All of the fruits of the sea are divided among the three water signs, the Fish to Pisces, the Crab to Cancer, and all other Shellfish to Scorpio. However, *all* of these are among the nouriture of Aquarius.

At the same time, the Aquarian fruits and vegetables are shared in common with Capricorn. As with your neighboring Capricorns, this offers the opportunity for broad complexity. Indeed, vegetables such as Beets, Eggplant or Zucchini may be prepared in a variety of creative ways.

Your fruits, such as Cantaloupe and Honeydew melons, may be eaten as picked or used as the centerpieces of elaborate fruit salads. Quinces, meanwhile, are one of the more exotic fruits associated with any sign of the Zodiac.

If you are an Aquarius of the First Decan, and you are intending to come into harmony with another person, use Licorice, Sage or Thyme to flavor the dishes of her or his primary sign.

If you are an Aquarius of the Second Decan, and you are intending to come into harmony with another person, you should focus on such flavorings as Bittersweet, Caraway, Clover, Dill, Fennel or Parsley. Peppermint tea is also effective.

If you are an Aquarius of the Third Decan, and you are intending to come into harmony with another person, you should focus on such

## AQUARIUS

*Fruits*
Cantaloupe, Honeydew melons, Quinces

*Vegetables*
Beets, Eggplant, Zucchini

*Herbs & Spices*

First Decan—January 21 through 30: Cardamom, Licorice, Sage, Spearmint, Thyme, Vanilla

Second Decan—January 31 through February 9: Bittersweet, Caraway, Clover, Dill, Fennel, Mint, Parsley, Peppermint

Third Decan—February 10 through 19: Cardamom, Licorice, Sage, Spearmint, Thyme, Vanilla, Wintergreen, Lemon peel

flavorings as Lemon peel, Licorice, Sage or Thyme.

Aquarians of both the First and Third Decan will note that Cardamom, used in the cuisine of India, is also one of your spices. You may be surprised with the results of a nice cup of Sassafras tea. And, also for both of you, a little Spearmint as a tea has wondrous potential, as does something as simple, yet sublime, as Vanilla Ice cream.

# CLAM CHOWDER

| | |
|---|---|
| 6 | medium potatoes |
| 2 | quarts cold water |
| ¼ | bunch parsley (a few sprigs) |
| 1 | medium onion |
| 2 or 3 | stalks celery |
| 1 | tablespoon butter or margarine |
| ½ | teaspoon thyme |
| 1 | slice salt pork, ⅓ inch thick |
| 4 | medium tomatoes, or 1 small can |
| 2 | tablespoons flour |
| 2 | dozen clams (or 1 quart) and juice |
| 1 | tablespoon Worcestershire or A-1 sauce salt and pepper to taste |
| 8 | soda crackers, or 2 pilot crackers |

Wash and peel potatoes; dice and place in pot with 2 quarts cold water. Wash parsley, remove stalks and chop the leaves. Chop onion very fine. Wash 2 or 3 outer stalks of celery and chop very fine. Add the chopped parsley, onion and celery, and now place pot over high heat. Stir in butter and thyme. Peel tomatoes, cut in small pieces and add. Cook until potatoes are nearly done. While the pot is coming to a boil, cut the pork into little pieces about ⅓ inch square, and fry in pan for about 5 minutes. Then stir in 2 tablespoons of flour, and add a cup of liquid from the pot. Mix well and empty all into the pot with the vegetables. Stir slowly to blend the flour and pork with the other liquid.

Open clams and place in bowl; strain off liquid into another bowl. Cut the clams in quarters, taking care that no shell is left in the clams. When the potatoes are tender, empty the clams and clam juice into the pot with the other mixture and stir slowly to prevent burning at the bottom. Boil for 2 minutes only, then remove the pot from flame, add Worcestershire or A-1 Sauce and salt and pepper to taste. Add broken crackers, stir slowly and serve. Serves 8.

# OYSTER SOUP

1 cup hot water
2 dozen oysters
3 cups cream or milk
1 teaspoon butter or
  margarine
  salt and pepper

Into a saucepan put hot water. Add oysters. Heat thoroughly, but do not boil. Be sure they are hot. In another saucepan heat the cream or milk. Combine with the oysters. Add the butter, salt and pepper. Serves 4.

# QUINCE AND HONEYDEW SALAD

4 cups honeydew
  melon balls
  pimento cheese
4 sliced quinces
  green pepper rings,
  chilled
  sliced stuffed ripe olives
1 cup mayonnaise
¼ cup pineapple juice
2 tablespoons lemon juice
½ cup whipped cream

Arrange a bed of lettuce on a plate. In the center place a mound of melon balls which can be cut with a vegetable cutter. Place 1 teaspoon pimento cheese in each center of the slices of quince. Arrange the slices around the melon mound. Decorate with the green pepper rings which should be chilled, and slices of stuffed olives. Serve with dressing of mayonnaise, pineapple juice, lemon juice and whipped cream combined. Serves 4.

# SHRIMP SALAD WITH MAYONNAISE

2 cups cold cooked shrimp
½ cup diced cucumber (optional)
6 tablespoons mayonnaise
1 head lettuce

Cold boiled shrimp should be used. Break the shrimp into pieces and mix with the mayonnaise. Diced cucumber can be added and mixed in with the shrimp, or it can be mixed into French Dressing (recipe on page 36) and served around the shrimp and mayonnaise on crisp lettuce leaves. Serves 4.

# BAKED STUFFED EGGPLANT

1 eggplant
4 tablespoons butter or margarine
1 finely chopped small white onion
2 tablespoons bread crumbs
1 pinch garlic
salt and pepper

Put whole eggplant into boiling salted water and boil until tender, but not too soft. Remove from water and cut in halves, crosswise, with a large sharp knife. Scrape out the inside but be careful not to break the skin. Heat 1 tablespoon of butter and add the finely chopped onion and allow to cook to a golden brown; then add the scraped egg plant, bread crumbs, salt and pepper to taste, and 2 very thin slices of garlic. Mix all these ingredients together well and refill the egg plant shells. Place 3 tablespoons of butter in a small baking pan and put in a 350° F oven; when hot, put in the stuffed halves of the egg plant and baste often with the butter. Bake until nicely brown. The top may be sprinkled with a few cracker crumbs and dabs of butter before being put into the oven to bake. Serves 4.

# BROILED EGGPLANT

1 eggplant
butter or margarine
salt and pepper

Heat a large kettle of boiling salted water. Boil the unpeeled eggplant in this for 15 minutes. Remove from the water. Slice in ½ inch slices. Place in a pan. Dot with butter. Dust with salt and pepper. Broil under a flame until a rich brown. Turn, dot with butter and brown the other side. The broiling takes about 10 minutes. Serves 4.

# BEETS IN SPICY SAUCE

4 tablespoons butter or margarine
⅓ teaspoon dry mustard
3 tablespoons tarragon vinegar
½ teaspoon sugar mace
2 tablespoons grated onion

1 tablespoon finely chopped parsley
2 teaspoons Worcestershire sauce
3½ to 4 cups cooked cubed beets
astrologically appropriate herbs and spices

Heat the butter in the top of a double boiler, adding the dry mustard, tarragon vinegar, sugar, a dash of mace, grated onion, finely chopped parsley and Worcestershire sauce. Bring to a boil, stirring frequently, and stir in the beets (cubed very small). Toss together and when well heated, serve in a heated vegetable dish sprinkled with chopped parsley, chives or other appropriate herbs and spices. Serves 6.

# OYSTER LOAF

4   soft rolls
3   tablespoons butter or
    margarine
4   cups oysters (1 quart)
    salt and pepper
    minced parsley
    Mushroom Sauce
    (recipe follows)
2   lemons
1   small jar salsa

Cut the tops from the rolls and set aside. Scoop out the center. Butter them inside. Put into the oven to warm. Drain the liquid from 1 quart of oysters. Heat 1 tablespoon butter in a large pan. Put the oysters in, keeping them separated. When the edges curl dust with salt and pepper. Fill the rolls with the oysters. Sprinkle with minced parsley. Put 1 teaspoon of butter on top of each. Replace the covers of the rolls. Heat at 400° F for 10 minutes.

Garnish with lemon cups. Pass the Mushroom Sauce (see below) with them.

The lemon cups are made by cutting the lemons in half. Remove the pulp with a grapefruit knife. Cut the edges with a fruit decorator or cut into points with a sharp knife. Fill with salsa. The bottoms of the lemon cups should have a thin piece cut off so that they will stand erect. A small loaf of bread may be substituted for the rolls. Serves 4.

# MUSHROOM SAUCE FOR SHELLFISH

½   pound mushrooms
4   tablespoons butter or
    margarine
1½  cups milk
3   tablespoons flour
¾   teaspoon salt
    pepper

Wash and slice the mushrooms. Cook them in 1 tablespoon of the butter in a covered pan. Do not brown. Make a cream sauce in the double boiler. Blend 3 tablespoons of butter, salt and a seasoning of pepper. Add the milk next. Place over hot water, stirring well as it cooks. Cook 10 minutes. Beat vigorously. Add the hot mushrooms to the sauce. Dust with pepper.

# ROASTED CLAMS

12 clams or 24 mussels
1 cup cornmeal
1½ cups melted butter or
   margarine
1 cup cooking wine
2 tablespoons minced
   parsley
2 tablespoons minced
   chives

Purchase clams or mussels in their shells. Wash and scrub them. Allow them to stand for several hours covered with water. Put the cornmeal in the water. This will insure a freedom from sand. The clams open the shell slightly to feed upon the cornmeal and this releases the sand which often collects in the shell. Heat the oven to 450° F. Place the clams in a pan with a rack. When the shells open they are done. This takes about 15 minutes. Drain the liquid from the pan. Strain it and serve in cups along with melted butter. Mussels are treated in the same way, except that they have cooking wine, minced parsley and minced chives added to the pan they are cooked in. Serves 6.

# FRIED SCALLOPS

4 cups scallops (1 quart)
2 tablespoons olive oil
   juice of 1 lemon
½ teaspoon salt
¼ teaspoon pepper
1 teaspoon minced
   parsley
1 egg
1 tablespoon water
   fine dry bread crumbs

Drain the scallops. Let stand in a dressing made with olive oil, juice of 1 lemon, salt, pepper and minced parsley. Let stand 1 hour. Beat the egg with the water. Dip the scallops in it. Then dip them in sifted dry bread crumbs. Fry in deep fat heated until it will brown a cube of bread in 1 minute (375° F). Use a fat thermometer to test the fat. Fry a few at a time until they are golden brown. (A frying basket is a convenience in frying foods in deep fat.) Keep hot in the oven. Drain on paper towels. Serve with strips of browned bacon, slices of lemon and parsley. Serves 4.

# PISCES

## February 20 through March 20

| *Ruling Element* | *Ruling Planet* | *Nouriture* |
|:---:|:---:|:---:|
| **Water** | **Jupiter** | **Fish** |

As a Pisces, you are introspective almost to the point of mysticism. You are as quiet as the sea, which has the potential for thunderous expression as well as quiet solitude. As with the other Water signs, Cancer and Scorpio, your nouriture is *of* the water. All of the fruits of the sea are divided among the three water signs, the Crab to Cancer, other Shellfish to Scorpio, and with all Fish to Pisces.

Your vegetables, which you have in common with Sagittarians, are Artichokes, Brussels Sprouts, Endives and Kale, and your fruits are Dates, Figs and Mangos. The figs may appear in desserts or complementing your main dish on the table's primary platter. Chestnuts may also be part of this presentation.

If you are a Pisces of the First Decan, you are the member of a very exclusive club. You are blessed as having been born during one of the four weeks of the year for which Tamarind and Tarragon are the only spices. Take them. May they serve you well.

If you are a Pisces of the Second Decan, and you are intending to come into harmony with another person, using the fresh flavor of Wintergreen is extremely potent, as are the oils extracted from the peels of citrus fruits, particularly Lemons and Limes.

If you are a Pisces of the Third Decan, and you are intending to come into harmony with another person, you should focus on such herbs and spices as Allspice, Basil, Coriander, Cumin, Ginger, or Pepper. Peppermint is also particularly useful.

As you are the least shy of Pisceans, you may also use Chili Pepper, Curry, Garlic, Horseradish or Mustard.

## PISCES

*Fruits*
Dates, Figs, Mangos

*Vegetables*
Artichokes, Brussels Sprouts, Endives, Kale

*Nuts*
Chestnuts

*Herbs and Spices*

First Decan—February 20 through February 28 or 29: Tamarind, Tarragon

Second Decan—March 1 through 10: Lemon peel, Wintergreen

Third Decan—March 11 through 20: Allspice, Basil, Chili Pepper, Coriander, Cumin, Curry, Garlic, Ginger, Horseradish, Mustard, Pepper, Peppermint

# FISH CHOWDER

5   cups water
2   cups peeled and
    chopped potatoes
1   minced onion
1   pound filet of sole or
    haddock
2   cups cream or milk
    salt and pepper

Boil 4 cups of water. Add the chopped potatoes. Cook 15 minutes. In another saucepan boil 1 cup water. Add minced onion. When the potatoes are done, add the onion. Lay on top of this the filet of sole or filet of haddock. Simmer for 10 minutes. Add the cream or milk. Heat. Add salt and pepper. Pour over biscuits and serve. Serves 4.

# BOUILLABAISSE

1   pound filet of sole cut
    in pieces
2   thin slices lemon peel
4   tablespoons butter or
    margarine
2   cups boiling water

1   small lobster or 1 can
    lobster meat
2   cups soup stock
4   tablespoons cooking
    sherry or orange juice
1   cup shrimp
1   thinly sliced onion
¼   teaspoon salt
2   tablespoons minced
    celery
¼   teaspoon curry powder
    juice of 1 lemon

Heat the butter in a pan. When hot but not brown add the filet of sole, lobster, shrimps, onion and celery. Cook in the butter 5 minutes. Add the lemon juice, lemon peel, and boiling water. Cook covered for 10 minutes. Add the soup stock, sherry or orange juice, salt and curry powder. Heat. Pour over slices of toast into hot bowls. Serves 4.

# ENDIVE SALAD

½ pound endive
5 tablespoons olive oil
3 tablespoons vinegar
½ teaspoon salt
1 tablespoon East Indian chutney

Wash the endive. Cut it into strips and chill. Dress with French dressing made with the olive oil, vinegar, salt and chutney. Arrange endive on salad plates. Beat the dressing well. Dress the endive with it. Serve with saltines spread with cream cheese and 1 teaspoon currant jelly in the center of each. Serves 2.

# BRUSSELS SPROUTS PISCES

4 cups Brussels sprouts
3 tablespoons butter or margarine
1 medium onion
⅓ cup chicken bouillon
salt
white pepper
cayenne pepper
chopped parsley and chives

Boil the Brussels sprouts in salted water for 10 minutes. Heat the butter in a frying pan; into this put the onion finely sliced in rings and fry until rings begin to turn yellow, stirring frequently, over a gentle flame; then add a scant ⅓ cup of highly seasoned chicken bouillon, and the cooked Brussels sprouts seasoned to taste with salt, white pepper and a pinch of cayenne pepper. Cook, stirring almost constantly, until the liquid is absorbed and the sprouts are tender but whole, not crushed. Serve sizzling hot sprinkled with equal parts of chopped parsley and chopped chives. Serves 8.

# RISOTTO PISCES

1½ cups rice
2 or 3 tablespoons salt
½ cup butter or
   margarine (¼ pound)
1 can anchovies or
   sardines
1 clove garlic
2 ounces freshly grated
   Parmesan cheese

Wash the rice in cold water. Fill a large pot with 2 or 3 quarts of water, adding 2 or 3 tablespoons of salt (1 level tablespoon per quart of water). When water is rapidly boiling, sprinkle in the rice and allow to boil until tender (about 20 to 25 minutes). Then strain and run plenty of water over it to wash out the excess starch. Put the rice into a dish with a clean damp cloth over it and reheat it in the oven, or place it in a wire strainer and place the strainer over the opening of a pot in which you have some fast boiling water. The strainer should cover the opening of the pot, so that the steam filters up through the cooked rice and heats it.

While the rice is cooking, put the butter into a frying pan and when hot put in garlic, chopped very fine, and the anchovies or sardines which have been chopped fine. Allow to cook until the fish disintegrate. Then mix in with the rice and serve with grated cheese. Serves 4.

# SALMON PISCES

4 salmon fillets
8 thin slices onion
   butter
   salt
   black pepper

Use the exact same method described for Sole Pisces (recipe above) to cook any fish. Egg and bread crumb should, however, be used only with flounder, halibut or sole. Slightly less butter can be used when the fish has not been dipped in egg and bread crumbs. It is important to brown the butter in the baking pan before putting the fish in—not just melt it, but brown it. This recipe may be used for trout, bass, perch, etc., as well as salmon.

Wash the fish by letting cold water run over it for a moment to wash off any loose scales that may be on it. It can then be dipped in slightly beaten eggs, then in bread crumbs and placed in a pan with the sizzling hot browned butter or, if using salmon, placed directly into the browned butter without the egg and bread crumbs. Sprinkle each piece with salt and black pepper and baste the hot butter over it. Bake at 400° F for about 15 minutes, basting once or twice while baking. Place 2 very thin small slices of onion on top of each piece of fish when baking.

In cooking fresh salmon, if it is a large piece and to be eaten cold, boil it, starting it in cold water with a little salt added after the water is boiling. Boil until fish begins to leave the bone. In cooking salmon steaks, broil under flame. These steaks are delicious hot or cold. Shad should be either broiled or baked in oven. Baking or broiling fish in browned butter is much easier because you do not have to turn it over. Simply put it in the pan and leave it in the oven until it is cooked, basting it once or twice while it is baking. Scallops are also excellent when cooked this way. Serves 4.

# SOUFFLÉ PISCES

- 2    cups cooked halibut
- 2    cups mashed potatoes
- ½   teaspoon baking powder
- 4    tablespoons butter or margarine
- 4    eggs
- ¾   cup cream or milk
      salt and pepper to taste
      other astrologically appropriate herbs and spices

Cook the fish and mashed potatoes, as in the recipe for fish cakes, mixing them together with the baking powder, salt and pepper. Beat well with a fork and add cream. Beat yolks of eggs until thick and lemon colored, add to fish mixture and stir in. When thoroughly blended, add the stiffly beaten egg whites and fold in as follows: Empty egg white onto the top of the fish mixture and cut down through it with the edge of a large spoon, bring the spoon along the bottom of the mixture and then up and over the egg white, cutting down through the egg white again. Continue to cut and fold, as this is called, until the egg white disappears into the mixture. Do not stir after egg white is added. Pour into deep buttered baking dish, place in a pan of hot water and bake at 375° F about 45 minutes, until the soufflé is set in the center.

# FISH CAKES

2 cups crumbled baked
    halibut or sole
2 cups hot mashed
    potatoes
1 tablespoon butter or
    margarine
¼ cup milk
½ teaspoon baking
    powder
⅛ teaspoon pepper

Boil potatoes and put through ricer. Chop the fish carefully, removing bones. Mix milk, butter, baking powder and pepper thoroughly with potatoes. Add to fish and beat well. Shape with floured hands into round flat cakes and fry in a little butter or bacon fat. When one side is browned, turn and brown other side. Or you may prefer to bake them as I do. Put 4 or 5 tablespoons of butter in a pan and place in a 425° F oven until the butter browns. Then put in the fish cakes, baste with the browned butter and bake for about 10 minutes. Remove from oven, baste butter over the cakes and serve. Serves 4.

# SOLE PISCES

4 filets of sole
½ cup butter or margarine
    (¼ pound)
1 egg
    bread crumbs
    salt
    black pepper

Wash the fish in cold water. Break the whole egg on a plate and beat it slightly with fork to thoroughly mix white and yolk. Place some bread crumbs on another plate. Dip the fish in the egg so that it is all covered with egg, then quickly lift it over to the bread crumbs and press the bread crumbs all over it. When all the fish is dipped in egg and bread crumbs, prepare baking pan. Place the butter into a large baking pan and put in 400° F oven to brown the butter. Watch carefully that the butter does not burn. Let the butter get not just melted but browned. This is very important. Take fish by the tail end and lower it into the hot butter. Then lift it and drop the other side in the butter. Do this with each piece. Then sprinkle each piece with salt and black pepper and place fish in oven. The fish will take about 15 minutes to bake. Baste every 3 or 4 minutes. When butter froths up on top of the fish when basted, then the fish is cooked. Remove from oven and baste until all liquid disappears into fish. Serve with baked tomatoes and mashed potatoes. Serves 4.

# FILET OF SOLE

1½   pounds filet of sole
     salt and pepper
1   cup fine bread crumbs
1   egg
2   tablespoons water
2   tablespoons butter, margarine or bacon fat
     Tartar Sauce (recipe follows)

Sprinkle the filet with salt and pepper. Dip in the bread crumbs. Then dip in the egg beaten with the water and dip again in crumbs. Heat the butter or bacon fat in the frying pan. When the fat is hot, cook the fish in this for 10 minutes or until brown on both sides. Garnish with parsley and lemon. Serve with Tartar Sauce (see below).

## TARTAR SAUCE

1   cup mayonnaise
2   tablespoons chopped parsley
2   tablespoons chopped dill pickle or relish
2   tablespoons chopped olives
1   teaspoon capers

Add the parsley, dill pickle or relish, olives and capers to the mayonnaise. Mix well. Chill and serve.

For additional seafood and fish recipes, see index.

# DESSERTS

essert is a special time of the meal and it is also a good occasion for a group of people of different astrological affiliations to come together to share several dishes and, at the same time, share the fruits of our own signs. Indeed, it is through the fruits of the Earth associated with our specific signs that we are able to express our astrological identities through dessert. The coming together is known as the Dessert Circle (or Dessert Zodiac).

Because of this, Taurus and Libra play an important role in the ritual and enjoyment of dessert. They also possess a special responsibility to take the role of hosting Dessert Circles, especially those involving the most common pies and tarts, such as apple, peach, cherry and those using various berries.

Pumpkin pie is, however, associated only with Scorpio and is a Scorpio cook's most important contribution to the Dessert Circle.

The Zodiac is divided between those signs for whom baked items are the principal type of fruit dessert, those for whom fresh fruit—such as a fruit salad—is most appropriate, and those for whom either may be appropriate. Indeed, when one factors in the likes of Cancer's Lemon Pie or the use of the Quince in pies, the distinction blurs, and any of the signs may fit into the latter category. Sagittarians and Pisceans, who were classically associated with dates and figs, also share the mango, which is traditionally eaten fresh, although we have given suggestions for its use with ham.

Finally, any of these recipes can be fine-tuned through the use of astrologically appropriate nuts, as well as with spices such as cinnamon, nutmeg or vanilla where they are astrologically appropriate.

| Baked Desserts | Fresh Desserts | Either |
|----------------|----------------|-----------|
| Sagittarius | Aries | Taurus |
| Pisces | Leo | Cancer |
| | Virgo | Libra |
| | Scorpio | Capricorn |
| | Aquarius | Gemini |

# BASIC PIE OR TART TYPES FOR EACH SIGN

**Aries:**
(Adapt Orange or Lemon recipes for Grapefruit, or use a fruit salad instead of a pie)

**Taurus:**
Apple, Banana or Banana Cream, Blackberry, Cherry, Huckleberry, Peach, Pear, Persimmon, Plum, Raspberry, Rhubarb, other berry

**Gemini:**
Pecan, Apricot, Pomegranate

**Cancer:**
Coconut and Coconut Cream, Lemon, Papaya

**Leo:**
Lime, Orange, Pineapple

**Virgo:**
Apricot, Pomegranate, Pecan

**Libra:**
Apple, Banana or Banana Cream, Blackberry, Cherry, Huckleberry, Peach, Pear, Persimmon, Plum, Raspberry, Rhubarb, other berry

**Scorpio:**
Pumpkin

**Sagittarius:**
Date, Fig, Mango, Mincemeat

**Capricorn:**
Quince

**Aquarius:**
Quince

**Pisces:**
Date, Fig, Mango, Mincemeat

# FRUIT SALADS

*See the following ingredients lists for your astrologically appropriate salad.*

Peel the fruits, slicing and removing cores, pits or seeds. Cut melons into balls or slice into 1 or 2 inch pieces. Peel grapefruit, oranges and/or tangerines and divide into segments. Trim away inner parts of skin and cut into sections. Remove seeds. Peel and slice pineapple into ½ inch pieces. Add berries or nuts and combine all ingredients into a bowl. Mix well. Chill and serve, garnishing to taste with astrologically appropriate spices. Serves 6 to 8.

### FRUIT SALAD ARIES

1  average watermelon
5  grapefruits

### FRUIT SALAD TAURUS

2  apples
3  bananas
2  pounds berries
   (blackberries,
   huckleberries,
   raspberries and/or
   strawberries)
2  ripe peaches

### FRUIT SALAD GEMINI

10  apricots
 3  cups chopped, mixed
    nuts (almonds, filberts,
    pecans and/or
    pistachios, but not
    including cashews,
    peanuts or walnuts)
 2  cups heavy cream

### FRUIT SALAD LEO

5   oranges and/or tangerines
1   fresh pineapple, opened and sliced, or one can of sliced pineapple
3   cups chopped, mixed nuts (cashews and/or walnuts, but not almonds, filberts, pecans or pistachios)
2   cups heavy cream

### FRUIT SALAD VIRGO

10   apricots
3   cups chopped, mixed nuts (almonds, filberts, pecans and/or pistachios, but not including cashews, peanuts or walnuts)
2   cups heavy cream

### FRUIT SALAD LIBRA

2   apples
3   bananas
2   pounds berries (blackberries, huckleberries, raspberries and/or strawberries)
2   ripe pears

### FRUIT SALAD SCORPIO

1   average watermelon
5   grapefruits

### FRUIT SALAD CAPRICORN

1   average cantaloupe
1   average honeydew melon
6   quinces

### FRUIT SALAD AQUARIUS

1   average cantaloupe
1   average honeydew melon
6   quinces
1   cup lime juice

# BUTTER DOUBLE CRUST

2 level cups sifted flour
2 teaspoons baking
   powder
1 cup butter or margarine
2 tablespoons sugar
¼ teaspoon salt
2 tablespoons cold water

Into a large bowl sift the flour, baking powder, sugar and salt. Stir around to mix these ingredients together thoroughly. Add butter and cut it into small pieces with a knife. Then mix the butter in further by flaking between the fingers and thumbs, going through the mixture until the butter is all in flakes and no lumps remain. Then very lightly rub the mixture between the hands, keeping the fingers stiff and slightly apart. Continue to lightly rub the mixture until the butter is thoroughly mixed with the flour. Now add the cold water and lightly lift the mixture around with your hand until it combines in one lump. (You might think that the 2 tablespoons of water will not be enough, but do not add more until you have lifted the pastry around the bowl several times. If necessary, add a little more water, but it should not be necessary.) When the

pastry dough is combined in one lump, sift a little flour into the bowl and turn the dough around in it. That will dry the surface and make the dough easy to handle. Divide the dough into two balls, one a little larger than the other. The larger piece is for the bottom crust. It has to cover the bottom and the sides of the pie pan. Now sift plenty of flour on your pastry board and in the center of the floured patch place the larger of the two pieces of dough. When taking the dough from the bowl, pat it slightly into a flat, round piece by lightly throwing it up a few inches from the right hand and keeping the left hand on top of it and patting it out flat as it falls back onto the right hand. Flattening out the dough in this way makes it easier to roll out without having cracks in it.

Roll the pastry to a ⅛ inch thick circle. Roll from the center out in each direction until the pastry is about 2 inches larger all around than the pie pan. Lift the pastry from the table by rolling it onto the rolling pin, starting it onto the rolling pin with the flat of a knife. Place the rolling pin on the pastry farthest from you and roll towards you, holding the last of the pastry onto the pin with the left hand while you lift the pin with the right. Place the edge that you are holding with your hand on the edge of the pie pan and quickly unroll the pastry onto the pan. Do not push the pastry down into the pan but lift the edges lightly and let the pastry sink into place. Now roll the top crust out all ready to put on the pie. Then put the fruit in pie. Both the top and bottom crusts should overhang the edge of the pie pan by about one inch all around. Turn the overhanging crust up on the edge of the pan and press the two together with fingers and thumbs of both hands. Press together and press slightly down. Continue to pinch it together all around the edge, one pinch as close as possible to the next, until the whole edge is pinched into a fancy border that stands up slightly around the pie and prevents any juice from boiling over into the oven. Prick the top crust in about a dozen places with a fork, or make a few small openings with a knife to allow the escape of the steam, which is very important. Makes one double crust 9-inch pie.

# SINGLE CRUST (FILLING AND PASTRY ARE BAKED TOGETHER)

1   cup sifted flour
1   teaspoon baking powder
1   tablespoon sugar
⅛  teaspoon salt
½  cup butter or margarine (¼ pound)
1   tablespoon cold water

Mix pastry as directed for the Butter Double Crust (recipe on page 108). Roll into a single circle of pastry. Place pastry in the bottom of the pie pan. Then double any overhanging dough onto the edge of the pie pan and pinch this with your fingers and thumbs all around the edge to make a fancy border. Do not prick the bottom of the pastry shell with fork. It is important that there are no cracks in the pastry shell. If there are, the filling will seep under the pastry, so carefully close any cracks by pressing together with finger tips. Fill and bake according to directions given with each filling recipe. Makes one 9-inch single crust pie.

# Baked Single Crust
## (Pastry shell is baked empty and the filling added later)

1 cup sifted flour
1 teaspoon baking powder
1 tablespoon sugar
⅛ teaspoon salt
½ cup butter or margarine (¼ pound)
1 tablespoon cold water

Mix pastry as directed for Butter Double Crust (recipe on page 108). Roll into a single circle of pastry. Place the pastry in the bottom of a pie pan. Then double any overhanging dough onto the edge of the pie pan and pinch this with your fingers and thumbs all around the edge to make a fancy border. Prick all over bottom and around the sides to prevent pastry from puffing up while baking. Bake at 425° F. Place the shell as close to the center of the oven as possible and bake until a creamy brown, about 12 minutes. Cool before filling. This recipe can be doubled or tripled and the extra baked crusts wrapped securely in plastic wrap, frozen and then stacked in a plastic bag for future use. Thaw completely before using. Makes one 9-inch single crust pie.

# Tarts (Various jams or fruits)

Mix pastry as directed for Butter Double Crust (recipe on page 108). Roll into a single circle of pastry and cut the pastry into twelve small circles about 4 inches across. The piece of pastry should be rolled to about 12 inches by 16, in order to cut twelve 4 inch circles out of it, but in case it doesn't roll to that size, you can cut as many perfect four inch circles as possible from it; then fill the remaining spaces in the muffin pan by putting in the scraps and pressing them together with your finger. Do not reroll. Then gently place these little circles over the ungreased openings in a 12 large cup muffin pan. Lift the edges and let the pastry sink into position. Gently press it first to the bottom and then around the sides, until it fits level with the top. It is advisable to rub a little butter around the cups in which the scraps of pastry are to be used, as this butter helps to join the scraps together. Remember, do not grease the other cups, because the little pastry shells will not hold their form but will slide down before they set. Prick the bottom of each little shell in two or three places with a fork to prevent air bubbles forming under them. Bake at 425° F for about 12 minutes or until a golden color.

These little pastry shells are delicious served with fresh strawberries which have been cut up in sugar and topped with a little whipped cream.

They can be served filled with any kind of stewed fruit or any of the fillings suggested for the cream pies. They are also delicious served with various jams and topped with whipped cream.

# FACE JAM TARTS

Mix pastry as directed for Butter Double Crust (recipe on page 108). Roll into a single circle of pastry. Place the pastry in the bottom of a pie pan. Then double any overhanging dough onto the edge of the pie pan and pinch this with your fingers and thumbs all around the edge to make a fancy border. The pastry can be filled with either one kind of jam or with two or four varieties of jam as follows: To make the tart with all one jam, just fill the shell about ⅔ full with jam. This can then be placed in the oven and baked until the border of the pastry becomes a golden brown. A more fancy looking tart can be made by rolling the scraps of pastry left over from making the shell into thin strips; then twist these and place them across the top of the jam, some in one direction, and some in the other, making a design of squares or diamonds over the jam.

To make a jam tart with two or four varieties of jam, use the scraps of pastry to build a little wall straight across the middle of the shell and another wall in the opposite direction. Then place various jams into each quarter and bake as directed above.

# SHORTCAKE

2 cups sifted flour
4 teaspoons baking
  powder
¾ teaspoon salt
6 tablespoons butter or
  margarine
¾ cup of milk

Sift into a large bowl all the dry ingredients. Mix. Then add the butter and cut it into small pieces with a knife. Then further work the butter in with the fingers and thumbs, squeezing the lumps into flakes. When the butter is flaked and no lumps remain, then lightly rub the mixture between the hands, keeping the fingers stiff and slightly apart. Continue to lightly rub until the butter (or other shortening) is completely mixed in with the flour mixture. When butter is blended with the flour mixture, add the milk and lightly mix it in by lifting the dough around until all the dry ingredients are combined. Then lift the dough with one hand and sift a little flour in the bowl, drop the dough and lightly turn it over in the floured bowl, so that the outside of the lump of dough is dry with flour. Sift some flour on the pastry board or table and into the center place the dough and roll out lightly. Finish preparing according to each recipe's instructions or roll out to ½ inch thickness. Place on baking sheet and bake at 450° F for 15 to 18 minutes. Serve with sweetened strawberries or other fruits and whipped cream.

# PREPARATION OF FRUIT FOR PIES

4   cups prepared fruit or
    rhubarb (1 quart)
1   cup sugar
1   tablespoon sifted flour
3   tablespoons water

If peaches are used, peel and slice thin. Remove stems and stones if plums or cherries are used. Remove small stems and thoroughly clean blueberries or other berries.

Mix the sugar and flour together thoroughly and put it into the bowl with the fruit. Stir it and add the water. Stir again once or twice. Make pastry as directed for Butter Double Crust (recipe on page 108). Pour the fruit into the pie crust. When the fruit is in the pie distribute it evenly and put the top crust on, joining the crusts together. Place the pie as near the center of the oven as possible and bake at 450° F for 15 minutes. Then reduce the heat to 325° F and continue to bake for 15 or 25 minutes according to the fruit that has to be cooked. Berries require very little cooking and will cook as quickly as the pastry. It is therefore not necessary to change the heat of the oven when making a blueberry, blackberry, red currant, raspberry, or other berry pie. When you can see the juice bubbling slightly through the air holes on the top of the crust, your pie is baked.

*For beginners:* An easy way to make apple pie is to stew the apples in a little water and sugar until cooked. Then chill the apples. Place the cold stewed apples and juice in a the bottom of a double pie crust, put top crust on and bake at 450° F until crust is golden brown (about 15 to 20 minutes).

# DEEP DISH APPLE PIE (LIBRA OR TAURUS)

1   *Butter Double Crust (recipe on page 108)*

2   *pounds cooking apples (should have enough apples when sliced to slightly mound in the dish)*

1   *cup sugar*

½   *teaspoon cinnamon, cloves or grated lemon rind, as preferred*

1   *tablespoon flour water*

Wash fruit. If using apples, remove cores and thinly slice. Make pastry as directed in Butter Double Crust (recipe on page 108), except use a deep dish pie pan instead of a regular size pan. Place in the center of a deep pie pan a small inverted cup. (This inverted cup serves two purposes. It acts as a bridge to hold up the pastry in the center of the pie, and it also draws up the juices in a way that will astonish those who do not know this old country tip.) Place the fruit in the pie pan, enough to slightly mound. Mix together the sugar and tablespoon of flour and pour it into the pan with the fruit (the flour gives a slight body to the juice) and stir it down into the fruit as much as possible. Now wash down the rest of the sugar from the top by pouring in slowly enough water to fill the dish one quarter full. Preheat oven to 425° F and place the pie as near the center of the oven as possible. Bake for 10 minutes, then reduce the heat of the oven to 325° F and allow to bake for 40 minutes in all.

# VARIOUS DEEP DISH FRUIT PIES

Follow directions exactly as if for Deep Dish Apple Pie (recipe on page 114), substituting any fruit for the apples. The following are excellent: Peaches (sliced), plums (whole), fresh cherries, red currants and raspberries mixed, apples with a few blackberries or huckleberries mixed or almost any other fruit.

Astrologically correct fruit pies are as follows: Apple for Libra or Taurus, Apricot for Gemini or Virgo and Quince for Aquarius or Capricorn.

# CREAM PIE (CANCER, LIBRA OR TAURUS)

1  Baked Single Crust
   (recipe on page 110)
3  tablespoons butter or
   margarine
6  tablespoons flour
2  cups milk
2  eggs
¾  cup sugar
1  teaspoon vanilla
   coconut or banana

Blend butter with flour. Heat milk in a double boiler. Add the butter and flour mixture. Beat until it thickens. Continue cooking, beating occasionally. Separate the eggs. Beat the yolks well and then beat into them ½ cup of sugar. Dip some of the hot mixture over them and stir. Then add to the mixture in the double boiler. Beat as it cooks. When thick and transparent remove from heat and cool. Chill in the refrigerator.

Prepare Baked Single Crust (recipe on page 110). Pour the filling into the crust. Beat the egg whites until stiff. Add 4 tablespoons sugar and flavor with the vanilla. Pile the meringue on top of the filling. Top with coconut for Cancer and banana for Libra or Taurus.

Brown quickly in a 500° F oven. This takes only a few moments. Watch carefully because long cooking melts the filling.

# BLACK CHERRY CREAM PIE (LIBRA OR TAURUS)

## CANNED CHERRY FILLING

1  can sweet black cherries
   (or white, if you cannot
   get the black)
½  cup sugar
½  cup cold water
1½  tablespoons cornstarch

Strain juice from cherries into small pot and add the sugar. Dissolve the cornstarch in the cold water, and add this to the juice and sugar. Bring this mixture to a boil and allow to simmer very slowly for half an hour. While the liquid is simmering, split the cherries in half and remove the stones, putting the cherries in a bowl. Then pour the heavy syrup from the pot over the cherries and chill.

## FRESH CHERRY FILLING

1  pound cherries
1¼  cup water
1  cup sugar
1½  tablespoons cornstarch

Wash and cook the cherries in 1 cup of water and sugar for 10 minutes. Strain the juice from the cherries. Dissolve the cornstarch in ¼ cup of cold water and pour into juice. Return juice to heat and stir constantly until it boils. Slowly simmer for 30 minutes. In the meantime split cherries into halves and remove stones. Then pour the heavy syrup over the pitted cherries, stir, place in refrigerator and chill.

## TO SERVE

1  Baked Single Crust
   (recipe on page 110)
   Cherry Filling (recipes
   above)
1  cup whipping cream

Prepare Baked Single Crust (recipe on page 110). Combine the pie at the time you want to serve it. Whip the cream until stiff and fill the pastry shell. Place the cold cherries and heavy syrup over the whipped cream. Serve.

# STRAWBERRY CREAM PIE (LIBRA OR TAURUS)

1  Baked Single Crust
   (recipe on page 110)
4  cups strawberries
   (1 quart)
1  cup sugar
1⅓  cup cold water
3  tablespoons cornstarch
1  cup whipping cream

Select one cup of the poorer berries, removing stems and washing thoroughly. Place in a pot with the sugar and one cup water. Bring to a boil and slowly boil 15 to 20 minutes. Strain through wire sieve, crushing the berries with a spoon. When all the juice is squeezed from the berries throw away the pulp and return the juice to the pot. Dissolve the cornstarch in ⅓ cup water and add. Stir constantly while adding until the mixture again comes to a boil. Simmer very slowly until it becomes a thick, heavy syrup. While the syrup is cooking, prepare the rest of the strawberries by washing, removing stems and removing the little white hard center from the strawberries. This can be done easily with a small, pointed knife. When the strawberries are cleaned and prepared, cut them into halves, or quarters, according to the size of the strawberries. Then pour the boiling syrup over them and put into the refrigerator to chill.

Prepare Baked Single Crust (recipe on page 110). To serve, whip the cream and fill the pastry shell with it, spreading level. Then place the cold strawberries and heavy syrup on top of the whipped cream.

# VARIOUS FRUIT AND JAM CREAM PIES

Follow instructions for Strawberry Cream Pie (see above) for all fresh fruits, blackberries, blueberries, raspberries, peaches, plums, ripe pears, etc. For all canned fruits, follow instructions for Black Cherry Cream Pie (recipe on page 116). Seedless grapes may also be used, but in that case use a boiled custard thickened with a little cornstarch.

# DUTCH APPLE CAKE (LIBRA OR TAURUS)

1½ cups sifted flour
3 teaspoons baking powder
¼ teaspoon salt
3 tablespoons sugar
4 tablespoons butter or margarine or other shortening
1 egg
⅓ cup milk
2 large tart apples
sugar
cinnamon
butter or margarine

Sift together the flour, baking powder, salt and sugar. Mix in shortening well, as follows: First cut the butter or other shortening into pieces with a knife, then squeeze the lumps into flakes with the fingers and thumbs. When the shortening is flaked and no lumps remain, then lightly rub the mixture between the hands, keeping the fingers stiff and slightly apart. Continue to lightly rub until the butter (or other shortening) is completely mixed in with the flour mixture.

Beat the egg slightly, add milk, then add to flour mixture to make a soft dough. Spread about ½ to ¾ inch thick in a greased pie pan. Peel, core and slice apples very thin. Place close together on top of dough. Sprinkle well with sugar and cinnamon and dot with small pieces of butter. Bake at 375° F about 30 minutes. Serve warm with whipped cream.

# BAKED BANANAS (TAURUS)

4 bananas
1 egg
bread crumbs
6 tablespoons butter or margarine
salt and pepper
lemon juice

Peel bananas. Cut them across the middle, and then through the center lengthwise. Dip in flour and then into beaten egg (beat the egg to thoroughly mix the white and yolk). Then cover with bread crumbs. Place about the butter in a roasting pan and place in oven. When the butter is brown, put the bananas in. Sprinkle with salt, pepper and a few drops of lemon juice. Bake at 450° F for 15 minutes. Serves 4.

# CHOCOLATE ALMOND CREAM (VIRGO)

1 cup milk
2 ounces unsweetened
    chocolate (2 squares)
2 eggs
¼ cup sugar
1 tablespoon powdered
    gelatine
2 tablespoons cold water
¼ teaspoon cinnamon
¾ teaspoon vanilla
¼ teaspoon salt
½ cup whipping cream
½ cup almonds
1 tablespoon olive oil

Soak the gelatine in the cold water. Cook the almonds in boiling water for a few minutes and then remove skins. Cut in pieces and brown slightly by placing in pan with olive oil. Place pan over medium low heat and stir almonds around until slightly browned. Remove from oil and allow to cool. Melt chocolate. Separate the eggs. Put sugar and egg yolks into the top of double boiler and stir to thoroughly break up the yolks. Add the milk and melted chocolate and cinnamon and cook in double boiler, gently stirring until the mixture begins to thicken.

Then remove pot from stove and add the soaked gelatine and stir until it is dissolved. When cool add the stiffly beaten whites of eggs, vanilla and salt and fold together by passing the spoon through the egg white, down and along under the mixture, then up and over the egg white again. When thoroughly blended, add the whipping cream which has been beaten until stiff with a rotary egg beater. Fold in. Now add and gently stir in the browned almonds and place the whole mixture in a mold. Put it in the refrigerator to chill. When set, serve with whipped cream. Serves 4.

# CRANBERRY AND PINEAPPLE PIE (LEO)

1 Butter Double Crust
    (recipe on page 108)
2 cups cranberries
1 cup drained, crushed
    pineapple
1 cup sugar

Put the cranberries through the food chopper. Add the drained, crushed pineapple and sugar. Prepare Butter Double Crust (recipe on page 108). Pour fruit into bottom crust and cut the top crust into strips. Then lay them over the fruit to form an open lattice design. Bake 10 minutes at 400° F. Finish baking at 350° F for 20 minutes.

# DATE PIE (SAGITTARIUS OR PISCES)

1 Single Crust (recipe on
    page 109)
2 eggs
¾ cup sugar
2 tablespoons flour
¼ teaspoon cloves
¼ teaspoon nutmeg
1 teaspoon cinnamon
1 cup cream
1 cup pitted dates
    coconut

Prepare Single Crust (recipe on page 109). Separate the eggs. Beat the yolks, add sugar and beat. Add flour mixed with cloves, nutmeg and cinnamon. Add to the egg and sugar mixture. Blend. Add cream and finely cut up dates. Beat the egg whites until stiff. Add to the mixture. Put the filling in the pastry and sprinkle the top with coconut. Bake for 10 minutes at 450° F. Reduce heat and bake 30 minutes at 325° F.

# LEMON MERINGUE PIE (CANCER)

1   Baked Single Crust
    (recipe on page 110)
1   cup sugar
1   cup boiling water
    juice of 2 lemons
3   tablespoons butter or
    margarine
3   tablespoons flour
3   eggs
6   tablespoons sugar

Put 1 cup sugar into the top of a double boiler. Add the boiling water and the lemon juice. Blend butter with flour. Combine with the lemon mixture and cook in the double boiler until slightly thickened. Stir constantly. Separate the eggs. Add the well beaten yolks and cook 10 minutes. Stir occasionally. Cool until cold. The pie should not be put together until a few minutes before it is eaten. Prepare Baked Single Crust (recipe on page 110) and cool. Pour filling into baked pie shell. Make the meringue by beating the egg whites until stiff. Add the 6 tablespoons sugar. Pile the meringue on the pie. Bake at 500° F for 3 minutes or less. Watch it closely and remove when a delicate brown on top.

# RAISIN PIE (GEMINI)

1    Butter Double Crust
     (recipe on page 108)
1½   cups seeded raisins
½    cup sugar
2    tablespoons flour
2    tablespoons lemon juice
     grated rind of 1 lemon
1    cup boiling water

In a bowl place the raisins, sugar and flour. Mix. Add the lemon juice, grated rind and boiling water. Stir and chill. Prepare Butter Double Crust (recipe on page 108) and pour the filling into the bottom crust. Cover with top crust and bake 30 minutes at 450° F.

# MINCE MEAT (SAGITTARIUS OR PISCES)

This is a quantity recipe to be made and kept for use when required in the making of Mince Meat Pies.

3 cups butter or margarine (1½ pounds)
3 pounds apples
3 pounds seeded raisins
1 pound currants
1 pound seedless raisins
2 pounds citron
2 pounds dates and/ or figs
½ cup candied orange peel
½ cup candied lemon peel
½ cup lemon juice
½ cup orange juice

2 pounds sugar (4 cups)
2 cups cider
1 teaspoon powdered cloves
1 teaspoon allspice
1 teaspoon cinnamon
2 teaspoons grated nutmeg
1 teaspoon almond extract
2 cups brandy
1 cup sherry
2 tablespoons salt

Put all the ingredients, except the seedless raisins and liquids, through a meat grinder. If you do not have a grinder then chop the ingredients very fine (but a grinder is best). Place all ingredients, except the brandy and sherry, into a large pot and allow to slowly cook for 2½ to 3 hours. Stir every now and then to keep from sticking and burning. Remove from stove and add the brandy and sherry. Keep in crock or tightly capped in mason jars. It is better if allowed to stand for about a week before using.

To make a Mince Meat Pie, use Butter Double Crust (recipe on page 108) using the Mince Meat for the filling.

# ORANGE PIE (LEO)

1 Baked Single Crust
   (recipe on page 110)

## MERINGUE

3 egg whites
6 tablespoons sugar
1 teaspoon vanilla

## FILLING

1 cup orange juice
3 tablespoons lemon juice
1 cup sugar
⅓ cup flour
½ teaspoon salt
1 orange rind
3 egg yolks
3 tablespoons butter or
   margarine

Add the lemon juice to the orange juice. Mix ½ cup sugar with the flour and salt. Grate in the rind of the orange. Add the liquid to the dry ingredients. Cook over hot water for 10 minutes, stirring occasionally. Separate the eggs and beat the egg yolks. Beat in ½ cup sugar. Remove the orange mixture from the fire. Beat in the eggs. Add butter. Cook for 3 minutes, beating the mixture constantly. Set aside and let cool.

Prepare Baked Single Crust (recipe on page 110). At serving time place the orange filling in the pie shell. Whip the egg whites until stiff. Add 6 tablespoons sugar and vanilla. Pile this on the pie. Set in a 500° F oven. Brown the top delicately. This should take 3 minutes or less. Watch the pie carefully or it will burn.

# RICH PUMPKIN PIE (SCORPIO)

1    Single Crust (recipe on
      page 109)
4    tablespoons flour
2    tablespoons cinnamon
1    tablespoon mace
1    level teaspoon cloves
2    cups brown sugar
4    cups mashed pumpkin
      or sweet potatoes
4    eggs
½    cup cream
½    cup melted butter or
      margarine
½    cup molasses

Using a large pot, put 3 inches of water in the bottom. Put another smaller pot upside down into the larger pot. Put over high heat. While the water is heating, peel, remove seeds and cut up a medium pumpkin. Lay pieces on top of small pot. If you are using sweet potatoes, wash and drop in whole. Steam until tender. Peel the sweet potatoes after steaming.

Mix the flour, cinnamon, mace and cloves with brown sugar. Add to the mashed pumpkin. Separate the eggs and beat in the yolks. Add the cream, melted butter and molasses. Fold in the beaten egg whites. Prepare Single Crust (recipe on page 109) in a deep dish pie pan. (This recipe will make 2 small pies or 1 very large pie.) Put into the oven at 450° F and at the end of 10 minutes reduce the heat to 325° F for 20 minutes. Bake until the custard is set. Whipped cream may be served on top of this.

# RHUBARB PIE (LIBRA OR TAURUS)

1    Butter Double Crust
      (recipe on page 108)
3    heaping cups cut
      rhubarb
1¼   cups sugar
3    tablespoons flour
2    tablespoons butter or
      margarine

Prepare Butter Double Crust (recipe on page 108). Mix rhubarb, sugar and flour together and pour fruit into bottom crust. Dot with butter. Cut the top crust into strips and then lay them over the fruit to form an open lattice design. Press edges together and trim. Bake in oven at 400° F for 10 minutes and then reduce to 375° F for 20 minutes.

# BAKED APPLE DUMPLINGS (LIBRA OR TAURUS)

Shortcake Dough
(recipe on page 112)
6 medium baking apples,
  peeled and cored
½ cup brown sugar
½ teaspoon cinnamon
1 teaspoon lemon juice
½ cup water
½ cup sugar

Prepare Shortcake Dough (recipe on page 112). Roll out until ⅛ inch thick and cut in six circles, each large enough to enclose an apple. Mix brown sugar and cinnamon. Stand each apple in center of a dough circle and fill the center of apple with the brown sugar mixture and sprinkle with a few drops of lemon juice. Wrap the dough around the apple and pinch together.

Stand the joined part of the pastry down. Place all the apples in a baking pan and prick the pastry with a fork to allow steam to escape. Pour into the pan a syrup made of the sugar and water. Bake at 400° F for 40 to 45 minutes. Pastry should be nice and brown and apple tender. You can test with a wire meat skewer. Serve hot with syrup from the pan. Serves 6.

# STEAMED PUDDING (SAGITTARIUS, PISCES OR GEMINI)

2½ cups soft bread crumbs
½ cup milk
3 eggs
½ cup finely chopped
  butter
1 cup brown or light
  brown sugar
1 cup chopped figs or
  raisins
½ teaspoon salt

Soak bread crumbs in milk. Chop the butter into very small pieces. Chop figs or raisins into small pieces. Use figs for Sagittarius or Pisces and raisins for Gemini. Mix all ingredients together and put

into a buttered mold with cover (or can be cooked in top pot of double boiler). Steam for 4 hours. Serve with cream vanilla sauce or with white wine sauce.

# INDEX

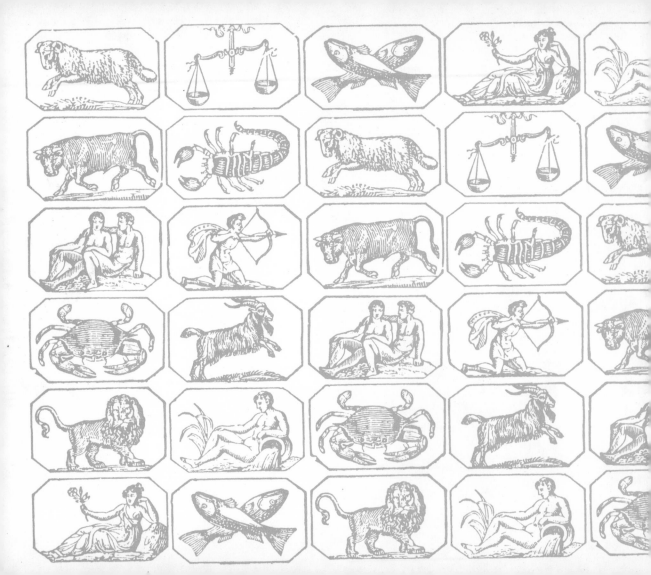